THE
IRISH BRIGADE

A Pictorial History of the Famed Civil War Fighters

Russ A. Pritchard, Jr.

PROJECT MANAGER: **Ray Bonds**
DESIGNER: **Jack Clucas**
PICTURE RESEARCHER: **Lang Picture Research**
U.S. GRAPHIC CONSULTANT: **Jennifer Houck**
COLOR REPRODUCTION: **Berkeley Square**
Printed and Bound in China

© Colin Gower Enterprises Ltd. 2004-02-18

This edition published in the United States in 2004 by
Courage Books, an imprint of Running Press Book
Publishers,
125 South Twenty-second Street,
Philadelphia,
PA 19103-4399

9 8 7 6 5 4 3 2 1

Digit on the right indicates the number of this printing

Library of Congress Number 2004 101011

ISBN 0-7624-2009 X

This book may be ordered by mail from the publisher.
But try your bookstore first!
Visit us on the web at *www.runningpress.com*

Contents

Introduction

Irish soldiers were found in armies around the world in the 19th century. Irishmen served in Napoleon's legions, in the Spanish army, in various South American revolutionary armies seeking independence, and in the Vatican's Papal Guard. Irish soldiers fought in the Mexican War, some on the American side and some on the Mexican side, and they also fought in the American Civil War, some in Union blue and some in Confederate gray. Later, Irishmen fought again on opposing sides in the Second Anglo-Boer War in Africa.

There were so many Irish soldiers in the English army that Queen Victoria finally recognized their contributions to the Empire by allowing the banned shamrock to be worn on St. Patrick's Day.[1] The Irish Guards, established in 1900, became a well-known and highly regarded 20th century unit of the Commonwealth armed forces.

It seems Irish soldiers appeared wherever there was a fight, no matter how remote the location and sometimes regardless of the cause. In many cases these Irish soldiers were considered mercenaries, men serving in the fighting forces of a nation not their own – and often rightfully so. Mass migrations of Irish in the 19th century, for economic, political and religious reasons, placed large numbers of this ethnic group in foreign places often hostile to them. Many Irishmen had prior military experience and, for want of employment, eagerly joined the military forces of their new homeland. It was not coincidental that most personnel, particularly enlisted ranks, of the small American regular army were foreign-born soldiers, but they were not considered mercenaries.[2]

The Eighth Census of 1860 determined that there were 1,611,304 individuals of Irish birth in the United States; some 1,526,541 of them resided in states that would remain loyal to the Union. These figures do not include those individuals of Irish descent who were born in the United States. The two totals combined substantially increase the number of Irish

stock in the country. It has been estimated that several hundred thousand Irish soldiers fought for the Union.[3] Irishmen alone made up the majority of at least twenty regiments of the boys in blue.[4]

This great influx of Irish immigrants was unwelcome to many Americans, and these poor people were frequently faced with the same discrimination they had suffered at home. They had to contend with strong anti-immigrant, anti-Irish and anti-Catholic movements in the United States in the 1850s.[5] They arrived primarily in the northeastern states, the closest landfall from Ireland, and congregated in the poorer sections of large cities. Most were penniless and uneducated, being unable to read or write. The Irish were forced to accept the lowest-paid and most menial employment as laborers and servants; the stereotype perception of the slovenly, drunken, worthless Irishmen was very pervasive. The overwhelming desire to be accepted drove many Irishmen to strive for that goal through valor at arms in their new country.

A substantial number of Irish had joined militia companies upon their arrival, for various reasons. After the Confederates fired on Fort Sumter on April 12, 1861, actually lighting the fuse for a four-year war between the states, the presidential appeal for 75,000 volunteers induced large numbers of these existing militia units to volunteer for service, and additional units were recruited.

The Irish volunteers were in the forefront of this patriotic endeavor. The 9th Connecticut Infantry, also known as the Irish Regiment, was raised in that state. Colonel John McClusky recruited the 15th Maine Infantry, made up predominately of Irish-Americans. The ladies of Aroostock, Maine, presented the regiment with a flag portraying obvious Irish sentiment on February 16, 1862. The obverse of the flag displayed the arms and motto of the state surmounted by a single white star, while the reverse bore the golden harp and green shamrock of Ireland.

Above: *Sunday Mass conducted by Father Scully at Camp Cass, attended by officers of the 9th Massachusetts Volunteer Infantry (the "Irish 9th") which was commanded by Colonel Thomas Cass in 1861. Father Scully is in vestments to the left of the wooden cross and Colonel Cass stands to the right. There is no question that strong religious beliefs played a major role in the behavior of Irish troops in combat, as evidenced by the fighting spirit and steadfast devotion to duty exhibited by so many Irish units. Although not all Irish soldiers were Catholic, priests were assigned to many of regimental staffs and accompanied the units in the field from the outset of the war. The "Irish 9th" was not part of the Irish Brigade but fought side by side with the brigade at Gaines' Mill during the Peninsula Campaign.*

Massachusetts formed sixty-two regiments during the war, the men including a large number of Irish soldiers who served in non-Irish or mixed-nationality units. The state furnished two regiments that were predominantly Irish. The "Irish Ninth," mustered into service in early June 1861, was the third three-year regiment (of the total of sixty-two) to leave the state for the combat zone. The other regiment, the 28th Massachusetts Infantry, eventually became one of the five regiments of what was to be called the Irish Brigade.

Small units such as the Emmett Guard of Worcester, a militia company, volunteered for ninety-day service at the first call and were already stationed in New York City by the end of April 1861. The 10th New Hampshire Infantry was the only Irish regiment raised by that state, although one other company, Mahoney's Company E, 19th New Hampshire, was predominantly Irish.[6]

The State of New York unquestionably furnished the most Irish soldiers of any state during the war, and New York City produced the majority of them. The 11th New York, the 1st Fire Zouaves, was almost completely Irish, and the 20th New York State Militia, with native-born officers, had mostly Irish enlisted personnel. The 37th New York, also known as the Irish Rifles, was obviously Irish, while the 63rd New York Infantry would soon become part of the nucleus of the Irish Brigade. The 69th New York Militia, the first to volunteer, would reenlist as the 69th New York Volunteer Infantry and also become a key part of the Irish Brigade. The 88th New York Volunteer Infantry likewise would join the 63rd and 69th regiments to form the nucleus of the Irish Brigade

Opposite page: *This magnificent gold-mounted, jewel-encrusted sword fabricated by Tiffany and Company, New York, was presented to Brigadier General Michael Corcoran by the City of New York at Suffolk, Virginia, on January 19, 1863. Corcoran's initials in diamonds on a blue enamel field adorn the counterguard, and the blade is beautifully etched with the patriotic sentiment "Never Draw Me Without Cause Nor Sheath Me Without Honor".*

Below: *Upon General Corcoran's return to duty he raised the Corcoran Legion, and the 164th New York Volunteer Infantry was one of the regiments in it. Colonel James P. McMahon, commanding, is playing chess in front of the headquarters tent. The regimental flag leans against the tent.*

throughout its existence. The 105th New York, the Western Irish Regiment, from around Albany and Rochester, was the result of recruitment of local Irishmen in that area. The Corcoran Legion, recruited wholly in New York in 1862, heavily Irish with some Germans, consisted of the 154th, 164th, 170th, 175th, and 182nd New York Regiments.[7]

The Commonwealth of Pennsylvania mustered a number of units that served for various periods. The 24th Pennsylvania, another of the 90-day units, and the 69th Pennsylvania, named to honor the 69th New York, was predominantly Irish. The 116th Pennsylvania Volunteers became part of the Irish Brigade for the greater part of its service, although it did not serve with the brigade during the last year of the war. There were a few individual companies like the Emmett Guards of Burlington, Vermont, that became Company A, 13th Vermont Infantry, an Irish company in a non-Irish regiment.

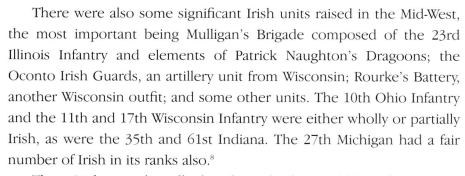

There were also some significant Irish units raised in the Mid-West, the most important being Mulligan's Brigade composed of the 23rd Illinois Infantry and elements of Patrick Naughton's Dragoons; the Oconto Irish Guards, an artillery unit from Wisconsin; Rourke's Battery, another Wisconsin outfit; and some other units. The 10th Ohio Infantry and the 11th and 17th Wisconsin Infantry were either wholly or partially Irish, as were the 35th and 61st Indiana. The 27th Michigan had a fair number of Irish in its ranks also.[8]

These Irishmen who rallied to the red, white and blue of the Union were remarkable men. As soldiers they exhibited a zeal for combat, obedience to battlefield orders, a steadiness in the face of fire, a cool indifference to death that was sometimes unnerving to other soldiers around them, and incredible endurance on the march. In camp few appeared on sick call and most maintained excellent health in spite of the unsanitary conditions that quickly struck other troops down with sickness – a testament, perhaps, to the immunities developed during years of living in squalor in Ireland.

Their quick wit, good humor and cheerful attitude enabled them to withstand the most rigorous marches, long campaigns and foul weather with gentle equanimity. Above all, they possessed a loyalty and pride in their unit that was truly extraordinary. They demonstrated this *espirit de corps* repeatedly in the most extreme combat situations.

Notwithstanding all these exemplary qualities, there was a dark side to the Irish fighting man as well. Most of them were illiterate but always had an opinion that they were ever willing to share, whether appropriate or not. Their appearance was generally not the spit and polish presentation required by the regular army. They appeared dirty and unkempt in camp, on the march and in battle, but their arms and accouterments were always clean and bright.[9] The Irish soldier was wasteful and careless with what he deemed unnecessary or excess equipment. Going into battle, he frequently discarded overcoat, blanket, knapsack and other encumbrances so that he could "fight light." The most serious problem was his notorious intemperance. The Irishman's overindulgence in any kind of alcohol was a continuous problem throughout the war, and probably was accentuated within officer ranks because it was easier for them to obtain.

During the war one participant familiar with the Irish soldier observed, "other men go into fights finely, sternly or indifferently, but the only man that really loves it, after all, is the green immortal Irishman. So there the brave lads from the old sod, with the chosen Meagher at their head, laughed and fought, and joked as if it were the finest fun in the world."[10]

Among these thousands of immigrant soldiers fighting for their new country were men such as Michael Corcoran and the aforementioned Thomas Francis Meagher (pronounced "Mahar"). These men would form and lead the famed Irish Brigade, the most renowned brigade in the Union Army, to the everlasting glory of the Irish soldier in the Civil War.

Chapter 1

Brave Irishmen All

Two charismatic personalities stand out in any study of Irishmen and the exploits of the Irish Brigade in the Civil War. One man has been called the soul of the unit, the other the heart. These men are Michael Corcoran and Thomas Francis Meagher.

Michael Corcoran was born in Carrowkeel, County Donegal, Ireland, on September 21, 1827. After receiving a good education he decided to go into military service, something of a family tradition. At age eighteen or nineteen, some six feet two inches tall, and weighing 180 pounds, he joined the British-sponsored Irish Constabulary, a paramilitary police force, and was stationed at Creislough, County Donegal. He soon became unhappy with the injustice to Irish people as he perceived it and in 1848 joined the Ribbonmen, an Irish guerrilla nationalist movement, while still in service to England's Queen Victoria. Eventually, he came under suspicion of treason and resigned from service. He quickly left Ireland and arrived in New York City in October 1849.

Young Corcoran found lodging and work at Hibernian House, a tavern across the street from St. Patrick's Cathedral. He was described as self assured but modest, calm, courteous and dignified. In August 1851 he joined the Irish Rifles, a company of the 69th New York State Militia, as a private and was soon elected orderly sergeant and then 1st lieutenant. He first saw Thomas Francis Meagher in May 1852 when the 69th provided a military reception for Meagher when he arrived in the city.[1]

Corcoran was elected captain of Company A in June 1853 and evidently married around this time. He became a naturalized American citizen in October the following year and was already very active locally in Irish politics. He found time to be elected to the post of school inspector in 1858 and was elected colonel of his regiment in August 1859. In just ten years the penniless, unemployed immigrant had become a recognized political leader within the Irish community, an elected school official, and a military

leader in the state militia system, and in June 1860 he was appointed to a well paying patronage job in the Post Office.[2] Michael Corcoran was living the American dream.

However, disaster struck in October 1860 when he refused to obey orders to parade his regiment; he was arrested and ordered to stand court martial. The beginning of the Civil War interrupted these proceedings and Colonel Corcoran led his regiment off to war. During the boring period in the defenses of Washington before the first battle Captain Meagher joined Corcoran's regiment and they built Fort Corcoran.

Eventually, the 69th New York State Militia was assigned to Colonel William Tecumseh Sherman's brigade in Brigadier General Irvin McDowell's army. Corcoran and his regiment performed gallantly in the Battle of First Bull Run. It was in reality a debacle for the Union Army, but Corcoran's personal bravery and that of his command gave the dispirited Union a hero when it needed one. The colonel was wounded and captured during the battle and sent south as a prisoner. He became a national hero again for his actions as a prisoner of war, refusing to be exchanged even in the face of summary execution.[3]

Colonel Corcoran was finally exchanged on August 14, 1862, and returned to a triumphal welcome. He was entertained all the way up the eastern seaboard, presented with a magnificent jeweled sword, promoted brigadier general retroactive to the date of his capture, and dined at the White House. It was reported that the parade and reception in New York numbered half a million people.

Unfortunately, his health had suffered considerably in prison. He had lost so much weight that he appeared cadaverous in a photograph taken in his new brigadier general's uniform. He also had no regiment, his old command having completed its term of service and the successor unit now being

Above: *Brigadier General Michael Corcoran in his new general's uniform as he appeared after thirteen months in several Confederate prisoner of war camps. At the beginning of the Civil War he was Colonel of the 69th New York State Militia and one of the leading Irish spokesmen in New York. His refusal to lead his regiment in a parade in honor of English royalty visiting New York City in 1860 had earned him a court martial and heroic stature in the Irish community. While under arrest he volunteered his services to the Union.*

under the command of his friend Colonel Meagher. Undaunted, in just three weeks he raised a brigade consisting of the 155th, 164th, 170th and 184th New York Volunteers that became known as Corcoran's Legion, or the Irish Legion, and was assigned to the Suffolk, Virginia, area.[4]

Brigadier General Corcoran and his new command performed admirably through late 1862 and the spring of 1863. As an acting major general he commanded the First Division, VII Corps, in North Carolina and participated in the Suffolk Campaign in 1863, before being reassigned to the Washington Defenses. Tragically, his wife died in July 1863, but he married a seventeen-year-old girl within a few months.

Corcoran and his division set up winter quarters at Fairfax Court House, Virginia, and invited Brigadier General Meagher, who was then without command, and his wife to visit and celebrate Christmas in "splendid style."[5] Then, on December 22, 1863, while riding with General Meagher on one of Meagher's spirited horses, General Corcoran died.

There are several descriptions of the incident that vary somewhat in detail. There is no question that Corcoran had never recovered from his ordeal in southern prisons. He was still weak. He and General Meagher had attended several holiday festivities and they both had been drinking. Some sources say the horse reared and fell on General Corcoran, while others say he threw up his arm and fell off. It is probable that he suffered a stroke caused by a combination of things. He was just thirty-six years old.[6]

Funeral services were held at St. Patrick's Cathedral, New York City, and the general was buried in Calvery Cemetery next to his first wife and his mother on Sunday, December 27, 1863. At a memorial service a month later at the Cooper Institute General Meagher delivered the eulogy.[7]

The Corcoran Legion was assigned to Major General Winfield Scott Hancock's II Corps after Corcoran's death. The unit fought well and hard in every campaign. After Cold Harbor in June 1864 it was essentially combat ineffective because of severe losses, but the surviving veterans served until the end of the war.[8]

Thomas Francis Meagher, like Michael Corcoran, was a native son of Ireland. Slightly older, he was born August 3, 1823, in the town of Waterford to a wealthy merchant family.[9] He received a good education at the hands of the Jesuit fathers at Clongowes and later at Stonyhurst, and early on developed an extraordinary talent for dynamic, compelling

Above: *Model 1850 Staff and Field Officer's sword presented to Colonel Michael Corcoran by admirers when he led the 69th NYSM to embark for their journey to the seat of the war in 1861. The sword was made by the Ames Manufacturing Company, Chicopee, Massachusetts. Originally, the sword was cased with a second ornate ceremonial scabbard adorned with Irish and American emblems, according to an article in The Irish American describing the presentation.*

Above: *Seated view of Brigadier General Michael Corcoran, probably taken at the same time as the full standing portrait on the preceding page sometime in 1862. His gaunt appearance is testament to the rigors of his incarceration that drastically affected his health.*

oratory.[10] As a young man Meagher was very active in Irish revolutionary affairs, participating in the Rebellion of 1848, and was arrested for sedition. He was tried, convicted and sentenced to death but the sentence was commuted to penal servitude for life in Tasmania, Australia. He escaped from there, however, and managed to get to the United States, first to California and then to New York, where he established himself in 1852, acquired citizenship, and became spokesman for the 'Young Ireland" group.

Upon his arrival he studied law under Judge Robert Emmett and practiced for several years before becoming bored. He started the newspaper *Irish News* in 1856 and published it with significant ability and honesty. By the time hostilities began he was a successful writer, lecturer in demand in certain circles, and a journalist, yet he immediately sought a military position in the regiment commanded by his friend Corcoran.[12]

In three days in April 1861 Meagher raised a company of one hundred men that became Company L, Meagher's Zouaves, part of the 69th New York State Militia commanded by Colonel Corcoran. He fought with the regiment in the Battle of First Bull Run, a shocking defeat for the Union Army. With the capture of Corcoran, overnight Meagher found himself in a position of leadership in the Irish-American military community.[13]

In the midst of political infighting he raised the Irish Brigade during fall and winter 1861-1862 and subsequently led the brigade during the Seven Days' battles around Richmond, and the terrible battles at Antietam, Fredericksburg and Chancellorsville. By mid-1863 the brigade had been reduced to a few under-strength companies because of staggering casualties. Meagher's pleadings with the War Department to be allowed to bring the depleted brigade home to recruit and refit fell on deaf ears.

Frustrated and despondent, General Meagher tendered his resignation and turned over command of the brigade to Colonel Patrick Kelly of the 88th New York on May 8, 1863. His papers arrived at the War Department in Washington, DC, on May 14, and Meagher went home to New York to await orders. On December 23 that year, the day after he witnessed his friend Corcoran's death, he received word that his resignation was refused, and he was ordered back to active duty. General Meagher was assigned to inconsequential rear echelon commands in Sherman's army in 1864 and 1865. He resigned again on May 15, 1865, at Savannah, Georgia.[14]

After the close of the war in 1865 General Meagher was appointed territorial secretary of Montana, and in the absence of the governor he was acting governor for more than a year. His life was unhappy and he was apparently paranoid of supposed enemies. On July 1, 1867, on a drunken spree at Fort Benton, Montana, he disappeared from a steamboat on the Missouri River. It is presumed that he fell overboard and drowned. His body was never found.

There seems to be strong circumstantial evidence that General Meagher was a chronic alcoholic. In his memoirs, Father Corby, a catholic priest who accompanied the Irish Brigade, noted Meagher's drinking on several occasions but says he was not a drunkard. The general's personal military secretary, Private William McCarter, 116th Pennsylvania Volunteers, notes "he (Meagher) had but one sin. It was the besetting sin of so many Irish then and now-intemperance."[15] McCarter recorded a particular incident that apparently occurred on November 13, 1862. While on guard duty he saw Meagher drunk and leaning against the headquarters tent, and saw him pass out. McCarter saved him from falling into a huge bonfire in front of the tent.[16] McCarter further states: "drunkenness in the army, especially among the officers, was alarmingly prevalent. The lack of success…of the Union Army might to some extent be traced (to it)."

> "I have not a word, other than that of unqualified commendation, to bestow upon this well-regulated and admirably disciplined regiment."
>
> Brig. Gen. Thomas F. Meagher

Below: *Hilt and upper portion of the scabbard of the Model 1850 Staff and Field Officer's sword of Colonel Corcoran. An Irish harp has been substituted for the letters US normally found in the guard decoration, and the whole hilt exhibits extra fine chasing. The white shagreen grip wrap is another special order item. The throat of the scabbard is engraved: "Presented to Col. M. Corcoran of the 69th Regt N.Y.S.M. in commemoration of the 11th of October 1860." This is the date of his refusal to parade for the Prince of Wales. A green Irish flag presented at the same time bears the identical sentiment.*

Below: *Colonel Thomas Francis Meagher, 69th New York Volunteer Infantry, resplendent in his dress uniform. His forage cap bears the numerals 69 and his non-regulation brocade belt has an unusual two-piece belt plate with eagle device.*

Meagher was away from his command often and sometimes without proper authorization. It is noted that he relinquished command to subordinates, sometimes for only twenty-four hours, sometimes for days at suspicious times. This occurred toward the end of the Seven Days' battles, and also after Antietam, after Fredericksburg and after Chancellorsville just before his resignation.[17] These absences may have been caused by what formerly was called battle fatigue and is now referred to as post-traumatic stress syndrome. The sight of the massive casualties sustained by his brigade may have been overwhelming to him. The sad circumstances of his death add credence to this theory.

General Marsena Patrick, Provost Marshal General of the Army of the Potomac, recorded in his dairy the most disturbing and vivid description of General Meagher during the siege of Petersburg in August 1864. For some reason Meagher was then visiting the 80th New York Infantry (20th Regiment New York State Militia), an Irish regiment known as the Ulster Guard. This regiment was serving as the Provost Guard at Headquarters, Army of the Potomac. General Patrick wrote Thursday night, August 18, "Genl. (Thomas Francis) Meagher is lying in the Tent of the Chaplain of the 20th as drunk as a Beast & has been so since Monday, sending out his Servant for liquor & keeping his bed *wet & filthy*! I have directed Col. (Theodore B.) Gates (commanding 20th New York) to ship him tomorrow if he does not clear out."[18]

Other Officers

A number of officers commanded the brigade at various times during Meagher's tenure and after his resignation, during the consolidation period and later after the brigade was reconstituted until the end of the conflict. Every one of them rendered valuable service and contributed to the legend building around the brigade.

"At the time it did not occur to one, but now, when years have passed and we look back we must feel astonished at the high moral standard of the army that fought the War of the Rebellion, and the Regiment was second to none in that respect. Seldom was an obscene word or an oath heard in the camp. Meetings for prayer were of almost daily occurrence, and the groups of men sitting on the ground or gathered on the hill side listening to the Gospel were strong reminders of the mounds of Galilee when the people sat upon the ground to hear the Saviour teach."

St. Clair A. Mulholland in *The Story of the One Hundred and Sixteenth Regiment Pennsylvania Volunteers in the War of the Rebellion: the Record of a Gallant Command.*

Above: *Brigadier General Thomas Alfred Smyth, who was commander of the Irish Brigade for only a short time in 1864 but was much loved and respected by the men. He was promoted to general officer in October 1864 and went on to commend a division.*

Below: *Brigadier General Marsena Rudolph Patrick, Provost Marshal General of the Army of the Potomac. Patrick served in this capacity under Generals McClellan, Burnside, Hooker and Meade. General Grant made him Provost Marshal General of all armies operating against Richmond in March 1865. Patrick was a strict, no nonsense disciplinarian with little time for incompetence or dereliction of duty.*

> "The officers of his command were, for the most part, men of superior education, gallant beyond any around them in the army; and as for bravery, this they imbibed with their mother's milk, yea, it was born in them. The 'rank and file' was composed of healthy, intelligent men, far above the average, and in many cases of liberal education."
>
> Father William Corby, *Memoirs of Chaplain Life*, describing men and officers of General Meagher's Irish Brigade.

Some had seen service with Corcoran and Meagher in the 69th New York State Militia. This was true of Robert Nugent, born in Kilkeel, County Down, Ireland. He served as a major and lieutenant colonel of 69th New York State Militia and subsequently led the 69th New York Volunteers. Nugent was in every battle with the brigade except Antietam, when he was absent sick. He was badly wounded and carried from the field at Fredericksburg. During his recovery he was acting assistant provost marshal of New York and commanded the remains of the Irish Brigade after Meagher resigned. Colonel Nugent commanded the brigade at four different times, the last being at Appomattox at Lee's surrender. He was made a brevet brigadier general after the fall of Richmond.[19]

Colonel Patrick Kelly was another officer who assumed command during several absences of General Meagher, and was in command after the general submitted his resignation in 1863. Born in Kerry, Ireland, and an immigrant to the United States, he joined the 88th New York Volunteers with the rank of lieutenant colonel during its formation in December 1861. He fought with the Irish Brigade at every engagement, through the reorganization, and was in command of the reconstituted brigade when he was killed in front of Petersburg on June 16, 1864.[20]

Irishman Richard Byrnes served as an enlisted man in the regular army for several years and in both infantry and cavalry units as a lieutenant early in the war, with considerable success. In late 1862 the authorities were desperately seeking a commanding officer for the 28th Massachusetts Volunteers, a malfunctioning regiment with little discipline or morale. The original colonel had been forced to resign for drunkenness and the lieutenant colonel had also resigned. Byrnes was appointed colonel over existing officers of the regiment on September 29, 1862, to the dismay of the regimental cadre.

Byrnes and the 28th Massachusetts joined the Irish Brigade just before the slaughter at Fredericksburg, where he and his regiment were the center element of the doomed assault.[21] He assumed command of the brigade on several occasions and was in command during the hard battles of 1864.

COMMANDING OFFICERS OF THE IRISH BRIGADE

Brig. Gen. T. F. Meagher: March 13 to June 28, 1862.

Col. Robert Nugent: June 28 to June 29, 1862.

Brig. Gen. T. F. Meagher: June 29 to July 16, 1862

Col. Robert Nugent: July 16 to August 8, 1862.

Brig. Gen. T. F. Meagher: August 8 to September 17, 1862.

Col. John Burke: September 17 to September 18, 1862.

Brig. Gen. T. F. Meagher: September 18 to December 20, 1862.

Col. Patrick Kelly: December 20, 1862, to February 18, 1863.

Brig. Gen. T. F. Meagher: February 18 to May 8, 1863. (Meagher was absent from command March 24 to April 26, 1863, in Philadephia and New York, for treatment of severe attack of rheumatism. He resigned commission May 5, 1863.)

Col. Patrick Kelly: May 8, 1863, to January 12, 1864.

Col. Richard Byrnes: January 12 to February 14, 1864.

Maj. A. J. Lawler: February 14 to March 25, 1864.

Col. T. A. Smyth: March 25 to May 17, 1864.

Col. Richard Byrnes: May 17 to June 3, 1864: wounded.

Col. Patrick Kelly: June 3 to June 16, 1864: killed in action.

Col. Richard Byrnes: June 16 to June 28, 1864.

2nd Brigade consolidated with 3rd Brigade June 27, 1864, as Consolidated Brigade 1st Division, II Corps.

COMMANDING OFFICERS OF REORGANIZED IRISH BRIGADE

Lt. Col. D. F. Burke: November 2 to November 5, 1864.

Col. Robert Nugent: November 5, 1864, to January 29, 1865.

Col. R. C. Duryea: January 29 to February 17, 1865.

Col. Robert Nugent: February 17 to June 25, 1865 (end of war).

Colonel Byrnes was seriously wounded at Cold Harbor on June 3, 1864, and died in hospital in Washington on June 12 with his wife by his side. He was buried in Jersey City, New Jersey. Colonel Nugent and several other members of the brigade acted as pallbearers.[22]

Thomas Alfred Smyth, from Ballyhooley, County Cork, served briefly as a commander of the Irish Brigade during the spring of 1864, when Colonel Byrnes was absent. Smyth served in a three months Pennsylvania regiment, and then the 1st Delaware Infantry until promoted brigadier general in October 1864. General Smyth has the distinction of being the last Union general officer killed in action, April 7, 1865, near Farmville, Virginia.[23]

After the war and the Grand Review the soldiers mustered out and returned to various walks of civilian life. Some immediately began to write of their wartime experiences while others would not take pen in hand for years. These memoirs published at various times have been instrumental in preserving and maybe even enhancing what has become the legend of the Irish Brigade.

The first man to publish a major work on the brigade was David Power Conyngham. He enjoyed a long career in Ireland and the United States as a revolutionary, novelist, war correspondent, Civil War staff officer, newspaper editor, government bureaucrat, and historian. His book, still considered the most important history of the unit, *The Irish Brigade and Its Campaigns*, was first published in 1867, has been reprinted at least four times since and edited as recently as 1994.

An Irishman who was born around 1825 in Crohane, County Tipperary, into a family of well off tenant farmers, Conyngham was educated at local catholic schools and then attended Queens College Cork but didn't graduate. He became involved in the "Young Ireland" movement and Rebellion of 1848, much like Thomas Francis

Opposite page: *The primary historian of the Irish Brigade, the dashing Captain David Power Conyngham, who served as a staff officer, at his own request, on General Meagher's staff, with no prior military experience whatsoever. General Meagher thought highly of his service and wrote a testimonial letter for him to that effect.*

Above: *Formal portrait of the officers and color guard of the 69th New York Volunteer Infantry, Irish Brigade, taken in camp near Washington around the time of the Grand Review. Lieutenant Colonel James J. Smith is seated center. Just behind him is the Second Tiffany flag of the brigade, brought down from New York to be carried in the Grand Review. The second flag from the left is the regimental National flag with unit designation and applied battle honors. Two officers on the far right wear mourning badges on their left sleeves for recently assassinated President Lincoln. Half a dozen of the officers wear II Corps badges on the left breast of the blouse. Many of the officers carry serviceable cavalry sabers or non-regulation European imported swords with metal scabbards.*

Meagher. He was indicted by English authorities but managed to disappear for several years. He surfaced in the 1850s and contributed articles to a local Irish newspaper. Conyngham wrote his first novel, *The O'Donnells of Glen Cottage*, in 1859. The story of a starving Irish family under English rule, it was reprinted several times as late as 1894.

He apparently first visited the United States in 1861 with the dubious credentials of a war correspondent for the newspaper *The Dublin Irishman*. In this capacity he visited the Irish Brigade during the Christmas holidays after the disastrous Battle of Fredericksburg in December 1862. Evidently, he announced that he desired to be an honorary member of General Meagher's staff and the wish was granted. Conyngham obviously served well in that capacity because Meagher gave him a letter to that effect, and he served as an aide with the rank of captain during the Battle of Chancellorsville. He seems to have left the brigade shortly after Meagher resigned and to have accepted an appointment as a war correspondent for the *New York Herald* in August 1863. He was really with the brigade for only about five months and took

> "It was a cheerful regiment, playing cards under fire, joking while actually engaged in file firing, and in camp ready for anything from a snowball fight to tossing pie peddlers in blankets, or driving a mule in full uniform into the Colonel's tent....They were a well drilled regiment, with clean brasses and muskets, even if they hadn't been able to wash for a week. They had no idea of being second to any other in anything."
>
> Colonel James J. Smith describing the men of the 69th New York.
> (Source: *The Irish Brigade*, by Steven J. Wright)

part in none of the major battles. Correspondent Conyngham accompanied the Army of the Potomac during the fall of 1863 and then was assigned to Sherman's army outside Chattanooga in March 1864, through the fall of Atlanta, the march through Georgia and the final campaign through the Carolinas.

After the war he joined the editorial staff of the *Herald* but spent most of his time writing about his wartime experiences. He published *Sherman's March Through The South* in 1865 and then began work on *The Irish Brigade and Its Campaigns*. For obvious reasons, he depended on other sources for much of the detail up through Fredericksburg and had Dr. William O'Meagher, one of the brigade surgeons who was there, write about the last years of the brigade. Even with these shortcomings, the book does great honor to the officers and men of the Irish Brigade,

Above: *Blood-stained maroon silk officers' sash worn by Major St. Clair Mulholland when wounded during the Chancellorsville Campaign. He received the Medal of Honor for his bravery.*

Above: *Wartime image of St. Clair Mulholland as a field grade officer. He served with the 116th Pennsylvania Volunteer Infantry in the Irish Brigade prior to Fredericksburg until the brigade was consolidated. After the war he became one of the champions for recognition of the accomplishments of the brigade.*

most certainly the objective. Mr. Conyngham edited several pro-Irish newspapers until his death on April 1, 1883. Quite expectedly, the Irish Brigade Association, veterans of the brigade he memorialized, gathered at the 69th Regiment armory in New York and eulogized him as historian of the unit.[24]

Father William Corby published his *Memoirs of Chaplain Life; Three Years with the Irish Brigade in the Army of the Potomac* in 1893, ten years after David Power Conyngham's death. Corby, a young Catholic priest, had joined the new brigade as chaplain of the 88th New York Volunteers to assist another priest, Father James Dillon, assigned to the 63rd New York Volunteers, in late 1861. Both men were sent out by a small Catholic boarding school in Indiana, later to become the renowned and respected University of Notre Dame.

Technically, priests were officers with the rank of captain but with no command authority. In many cases they were considered a nuisance, at best tolerated, but Father Corby seems to have been a notable exception. He had the opportunity to observe General Meagher in the formative days of the brigade and was present on the firing line in major engagements. He was by no means an "only on Sunday," rear echelon spiritual advisor, and he stayed on long after Meagher left.

Father Corby is best known in Civil War circles for the incident that occurred on July 2, 1863, the second day of the Battle of Gettysburg, when quite spontaneously he granted absolution to the whole brigade in the midst of battle as they were going into action in the Wheatfield. The act is the subject of the painting *Absolution Under Fire* by Paul Henry Wood, done in 1891. Father Corby stayed with the brigade until the siege of Petersburg in 1864 when he was called back to Notre Dame, but returned to the unit briefly in February 1865. He became the third president of Notre Dame in 1866 and devoted himself to building the school.

Then, in 1888, he received an invitation to the 25th anniversary commemoration of the Battle of Gettysburg and a reunion of the veterans of the Irish Brigade. Here he renewed his friendship with Brevet Brigadier General St. Clair A. Mulholland, former colonel of the 116th Pennsylvania Volunteers, and his old comrades in arms of the brigade. One of the results became his desire to publish his memoirs of the time he spent with these men, which he did a few years later. Father Corby's book was well received, particularly by his comrades, and has remained a cornerstone of literature concerning the Irish Brigade. Like Conyngham's book, it has been republished and recently edited in a scholarly manner by Lawrence Frederick Kohl in his on-going efforts to tell the story of the famous unit of the Army of the Potomac.

General Mulholland published his memoirs, *The Story of the 116th Regiment, Pennsylvania Volunteers*, in 1903, six years after Father

continued on page 22

THE MEDAL OF HONOR

The first Army Medal of Honor was authorized July 12, 1862. During the war a total of 1,196 Medals of Honor were awarded to Army personnel, at least 74 of which were of Irish birth and 6 served in the Irish Brigade.

Irish Brigade Recipients of the Medal of Honor

Major St. Clair Mulholland, 116th Pennsylvania Infantry, Chancellorsville, Virginia, May 4-5, 1863. Citation: In command of the picket line, held the enemy in check all night to cover the retreat of the Army.

Major James Quinlan, 88th New York Infantry, Savage Station, Virginia, June 29, 1862. Citation: Led his regiment on the enemy's battery, silenced the guns, held the position against overwhelming numbers, and covered the retreat of the 2nd Army Corps.

1st Lieutenant George W. Ford, Company E, 88th New York Infantry, Sayler's Creek, Virginia, April 6, 1865. Citation: Capture of (Confederate) flag.

1st Lieutenant Louis J. Sacriste, Company D, 116th Pennsylvania Infantry, Chancellorsville, Virginia, May 5, 1863, Auburn, Virginia, October 14, 1863. Citation: Saved from capture a gun of the 5th Maine Battery. Voluntarily carried orders which resulted in saving from destruction or capture the picket line of the 1st Division, 2nd Corps.

Private Timothy Donoghue, Company B, 69th New York Infantry, Fredericksburg, Virginia, December 13, 1862. Citation: Voluntarily carried a wounded officer off the field from between the lines; while doing this he was himself wounded.

Private Peter Rafferty, Company B, 69th New York Infantry, Malvern Hill, Virginia, July 1, 1862. Citation: Having been wounded and directed to the rear, declined to go, but continued in action, receiving several additional wounds, which resulted in his capture by the enemy and his total disability for military service.

SOURCES:

Manning, Robert, *Above and Beyond, A History of the Medal of Honor from the Civil War to Vietnam,* Boston, Boston Publishing Company, 1985.

U.S. War Department, *The War of the Rebellion, A Compilation of the Official Records of the Union and Confederate Armies,* 128 vols. Washington, DC, U.S. Government Printing Office, 1880-1901, Series 1, Vol. 46, Part One, pgs 1257-1261.

Citation source: www.army.mil/cmh-pg/mohciv.htm

Below: *1st Lieutenant George W. Ford, 88th New York Volunteer Infantry and Medal of Honor recipient, photographed in camp near Washington around the time of the Grand Review in 1865. Lieutenant Ford wears a mourning badge for assassinated President Lincoln on the left sleeve of his unusual custom-tailored, velvet collared, double-breasted, four-button sack coat, and carries a cavalry saber rather than the proscribed infantry foot officer's sword, typical of the wide latitude of dress permitted for officers.*

Corby's death. His book is pertinent to the time that his regiment served with the brigade, October 1862 through the reorganization until June 1864. Mulholland joined 116th Pennsylvania as lieutenant colonel during its formation in Philadelphia. Losses at Fredericksburg forced the regiment to be consolidated into four companies, and Mulholland was reduced in rank to major.

With this rank he commanded the battalion at Chancellorsville, May 3-4, 1863, and was awarded the Medal of Honor for his command of the rear guard of the Army of the Potomac during the subsequent retreat. He was made a brevet brigadier general, and after the war served as sheriff of Philadelphia. He was grand marshal of many a Memorial Day parade, and was active in postwar years with all veterans, particularly those of the Irish Brigade, and with the establishment of the present day battlefield at Gettysburg. His book, too, has been reprinted, including one edited by Lawrence Frederick Kohl in 1996. Mulholland's description of Father Corby giving absolution at Gettysburg is considered the most accurate and most moving of all the remembrances of the event.

Perhaps the most fascinating and detailed reminiscence of the brigade is that by an enlisted man, Private William McCarter, who served under Mulholland. He is the only man from the ranks to so document his service with the brigade. McCarter was born in Derry, Ireland, in 1840 or 1841, and by the time of the war, with a wife and several children, was employed as a hide tanner in Philadelphia. Unfortunately, McCarter served only briefly, receiving multiple wounds during the assault of Marye's Heights, Fredericksburg, but, as Meagher's personal secretary, he had the opportunity to observe the general closely. His education and intellect allowed him to be incredibly descriptive of conditions and events immediately surrounding him. His astute eye for detail and ability to chronicle events clearly make interesting reading. Astonishingly, his manuscript was basically unpublished until 1996 when Kevin O'Brien presented Irish Brigade enthusiasts with McCarter's *My Life in the Irish Brigade*. Some of his descriptions of the dead and the dying are unforgettable, and reading his narrative of the assault of his regiment at Fredericksburg is as close to being there as one can get.

These are the men who led or fought with the Irish Brigade on its journey to fame and glory, and the men who wrote about the unit to insure that the soldiers' deeds would not be quickly forgotten as years passed and memories dimmed. The continuing interest in and fascination with this colorful military organization is positive proof that they have been eminently successful.

IRISH-BORN MEDAL OF HONOR RECIPIENTS FROM OTHER UNITS

Assistant Surgeon Bernard Irwin, U. S. Army

Captain John Lonergan, 13th Vermont Infantry

Lieutenant James Gribben, 2nd New York Cavalry

Lieutenant Charles McAnally, 69th Pennsylvania
    Infantry

Sergeant Major Augustus Barry, 16th U. S. Infantry

Sergeant Major Joseph Keele, 182nd New York
    Infantry

Color Sergeant George McKee, 89th New York
    Infantry

First Sergeant Patrick Irwin, 14th Michigan Infantry

First Sergeant William Jones, 73rd New York Infantry

First Sergeant Thomas J. Murphy, 146th New York
    Infantry

Sergeant Terrance Begley, 7th New York Heavy
    Artillery

Sergeant John Brosnan, 164th New York Infantry

Sergeant Hugh Carey, 82nd New York Infantry

Sergeant Richard Gasson, 47th New York Infantry

Sergeant John Havron, 1st Rhode Island Infantry

Sergeant Patrick McEnroe, 6th New York Cavalry

Sergeant Thomas McGraw, 5th U. S. Artillery

Sergeant Dennis J. F. Murphy, 14th Wisconsin
    Infantry

Sergeant John Nolen, 8th New Hampshire Infantry

Sergeant William Toomer, 127th Illinois Infantry

Chief Bugler Thomas Wells, 6th New York Cavalry

Corporal James Cullen, 82nd New York Infantry

Corporal Patrick Doody, 164th New York Infantry

Corporal Christopher Flynn, 14th Connecticut
    Infantry

Corporal Patrick Highland, 23rd Illinois Infantry

Corporal John Kane, 100th New York Infantry

Corporal John Keough, 67th Pennsylvania Infantry

Corporal Peter McAdams, 98th Pennsylvania Infantry

Corporal Owen McGrough, 5th U. S. Artillery

Corporal Alexander McHale, 26th Michigan Infantry

Corporal Patrick Monaghan, 48th Pennsylvania
    Infantry

Corporal Thomas C. Murphy, 31st Illinois Infantry

Corporal George Tyrell, 5th Ohio Infantry

Corporal John Walsh, 5th New York Cavalry

Corporal Richard Welch, 37th Massachusetts Infantry

Private Felix Branagan, 74th New York Infantry

Private Michael Burk, 125th New York Infantry

Private William Campbell, 30th Ohio Infantry

Private David Casey, 25th Massachusetts Infantry

Private James Connors, 43rd New York Infantry

Private William Cosgrove, 30th Massachusetts
    Infantry

Private John Creed, 23rd Illinois Infantry

Private William Downey, 4th Massachusetts Cavalry

Private Thomas Fallon, 37th New York Infantry

Private Patrick Ginley, 1st New York Light Artillery

Private Thomas Kelly, 6th U. S. Cavalry

Private John Kennedy, 2nd U. S. Artillery

Private Richard Mangum, 148th New York Infantry

Private Bernard McCarren, 1st Delaware Infantry

Private Patrick McGuire, Chicago Mercantile Battery,
    Illinois Light Artillery

Private Michael McKeever, 5th Pennsylvania Cavalry

Private John Murphy, 5th Ohio Cavalry

Private Peter O'Brien, 1st New York Cavalry

Private Timothy O'Connor, 1st U. S. Cavalry

Private George C. Platt, 6th U. S. Cavalry

Private Thomas Riley, 1st Louisiana Cavalry

Private John Robinson, 19th Massachusetts Infantry

Private Thomas Robinson, 81st Pennsylvania Infantry

Private Peter Ryan, 11th Indiana Infantry

Private Patrick Scanlon, 4th Massachusetts Cavalry

Private Timothy Spilane, 16th Pennsylvania Cavalry

Private Bernard Shields, 2nd West Virginia Cavalry

Private Joseph Stewart, 1st Maryland Infantry

Private M. Emmett Urell, 82nd New York Infantry

Private Edward Welsh, 54th Ohio Infantry

Private James Welsh, 4th Rhode Island Infantry

Private Christopher Wilson, 73rd New York Infantry

Private Robert Wright, 14th U. S. Infantry

*Source: The Medal of Honor of the United States
Army, Washington, DC, Government Printing
Office, 1948.*

*Note: Irish born soldiers whose place of birth was
not recorded on enlistment papers and American
citizens of Irish ancestry who received the Medal
of Honor are not included on this list.*

Chapter 2

Uniforms, Weapons, and Equipment

What we know of the uniforms, weapons, and equipment of the Civil War soldier largely comes from examination and interpretation of period photographs and contemporary literary descriptions, relevant regulations, and actual examples in museums or private collections. Obviously most of the uniforms seen in period images were specially worn for the purpose of having the subject's image made for friends and admirers, and thus do not illustrate what was necessarily worn during campaigns in the field. Descriptions in diaries, letters and newspapers of the period are usually short and nonspecific in nature unless the item being described is particularly unusual or drastically different from the norm, such as the green flags of the Irish Brigade.

Colonel Michael Corcoran and Captain, subsequently Acting Major, Thomas Francis Meagher began their Civil War military careers together in the 69th New York State Militia. Colonel Corcoran commanded the regiment when it left New York until his capture during the Battle of First Bull Run, July 23, 1861. Captain Meagher was senior officer of what was known as Meagher's Zouaves – Company K of that regiment – and later acting major on Corcoran's staff at the Battle of First Bull Run.

During this period Colonel Corcoran was photographed on several occasions. In a series of studio photographs he wore a regulation dark blue, double-breasted, seven-button frock coat with knee length skirt and oversize colonel's shoulder straps; light blue kersey trousers with a one-inch dark stripe, probably red, down the outseam; and a forage cap with, on the front, officers' insignia that appears to be a wreath surrounding two letters, either NY or US.[1]

In another photograph, a group image taken in the summer of 1861 at Fort Corcoran, one of the forts in the defenses of Washington, the colonel is pictured with a dark forage cap with gold lace on the band and sides of the cap, a dark blue, double-breasted, long frock coat, and dark blue trousers. He wears a non-regulation baldric box with bullion-striped shoulder strap with stamped brass insignia affixed over his left shoulder diagonally across his chest, and dark leather waist belt with non-regulation eagle belt plate and sword of indeterminable type.[2] The other officers in the

Below: *Colonel Michael Corcoran and the officers of the 69th New York State Militia gather around an artillery piece at Fort Corcoran, a major earthwork fortification in the defensive perimeter of Washington, in 1861. Colonel Corcoran, far left, wears a non-regulation Baldric box on a brocade shoulder strap across his left shoulder, as does the portly, bearded officer on the far right. This fancy accouterment was in favor with militia officers during the period. Corcoran also wears a non-regulation sword belt plate. The medical officer, front, fifth from the right, carries a standard Model 1840 Medical Officer's Sword on a non-regulation belt with two-piece belt plate. The officer second from the right, possibly a paymaster, has a small, non-issue revolver in a holster on his sword belt. Most officers appear to have correct regulation uniforms and side arms.*

photograph appear to wear regulation uniforms appropriate for rank and branch of service and carry regulation swords of varying types.

In a photograph made in 1861 Captain Meagher is shown wearing a pleated, single-breasted, dark blue over-blouse that comes down to the upper thigh, much like the uniform known as the Burnside Pattern which this may well be. The sleeves button at the wrist and the large collar is folded down. A white shirt collar and black cravat show at the neck. He wears standard shoulder straps in the proscribed manner on the blouse. Meagher carries a Model 1850 foot officers' sword appropriate for his rank attached to a black leather sword belt with rectangular sword belt plate, possibly with letters NY within a silver wreath affixed to it. He wears dark trousers, probably the same color as his blouse, interestingly turned up at the ankle. The type of footgear is not discernible and no headgear is apparent.[3]

This uniform is not the one he wore as captain of Company K, Meagher's Zouaves, at First Bull Run. Meagher and his company did not wear full zouave uniform, only a short open blue jacket with red tombeaux and trim, vest and emerald green sash, blue trousers with

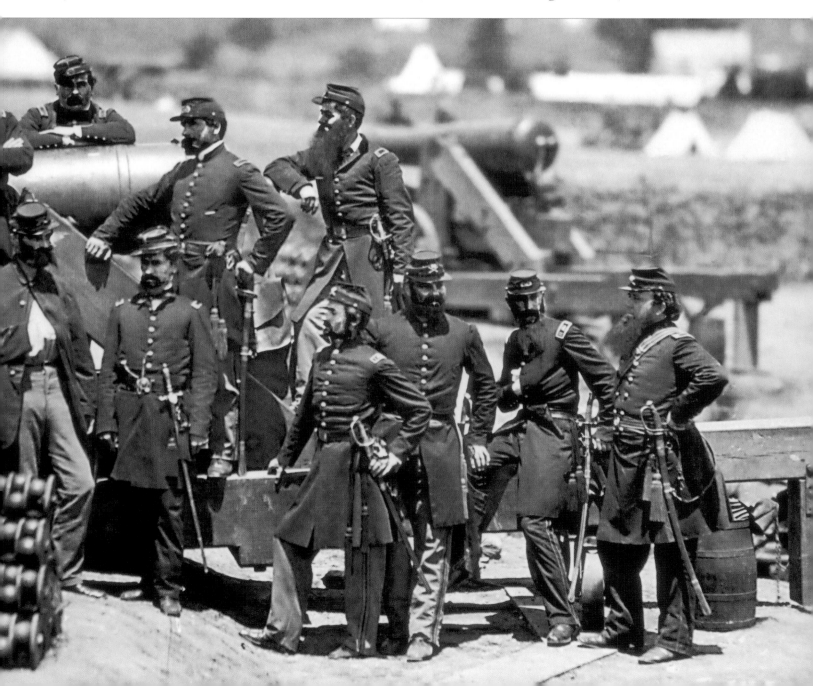

"On Wednesday, September 17, 1862, General Meagher, gotten up most gorgeously in a somewhat fancy uniform, with a gold shoulder-belt, was carefully brushed by an orderly, and remarked that 'we'd all have a brush soon.' We had it."

Colonel James J. Smith in a history of the 69th New York. (Source: *The Irish Brigade*, by Steven J. Wright)

narrow red welt on the outseam, and a low-crown, chasseur's style forage cap with stamped brass numerals 69 on the front of the hat. Conyngham comments on Meagher's Zouaves: "Meagher's company of Zouave suffered desperately, their red dress making them a conspicuous marks for the enemy." Meagher and the other officers wore similar uniforms with gold lace on their jackets and crimson and gold stripes on their trousers.[4]

Meagher was subsequently photographed in the uniform of a colonel during the period that he was commanding officer of the 69th New York Volunteers. In that photograph he wears the regulation seven-button, double-breasted frock coat with large shoulder straps, and a forage cap with gold lace trim. He has a non-regulation waist belt, probably covered in gold bullion lace, with an unusual two-piece interlocking belt plate with eagle device. On occasion, Meagher is also known to have worn a militia style baldric box similar in style to that worn by Colonel Corcoran.

Brigadier General Meagher was also photographed in the regulation uniform for an officer of that rank. In that picture he wears a double-breasted, dark blue frock coat with two rows of eight buttons arranged in groups of two, and black velvet cuffs and collar. The single star shoulder straps are regulation size, not the oversize variation often seen on Irish Brigade officers, nor is there any other ostentatious adornment on the uniform. Various descriptions of his dress and that of his immediate staff indicate that they all generally wore especially fine uniforms with extra gilt and gold lace, but this is not the case in this image.[5] General Meagher is also described as wearing a green velvet suit at Savage Station during the Seven Days'.[6]

Uniforms of the other officers and enlisted personnel of the Irish Brigade differed little from those of other units of the Army of the Potomac and the Federal army in general. Basically, soldiers of the Irish Brigade wore the appropriate regulation uniform then in use. As was the custom in every unit, there was noticeable latitude in the dress allowed for officers.

Above: *Captain Thomas Francis Meagher in 1861 as a new company grade officer in the 69th NYSM wearing one of his typical totally non-regulation uniforms.*

Opposite page: *Study of the uniform worn by Company K, the Irish Zouaves, 69th New York State Militia, at the battle of First Bull Run. Captain Meagher commanded the company but was acting major, a staff officer for Colonel Corcoran, during the engagement.*

Officers' Hats and Caps

Officers' headgear generally were variations of the forage cap and slouch hat. Some examples evident in period photography appear to be quartermaster regulation, while others exhibit considerable individual taste. There seem to be both low-crown chasseur and high floppy-crown styles of the forage cap. No Pattern 1858 Hardee hats have been observed in photographs of Irish Brigade officers or enlisted ranks. The soft-crowned slouch hat with officers' hat cords and a crease down the center seems to have been preferred and have been noted with corps badges affixed to the left side of the body of the hat with branch insignia on the front.[7]

Officers' Hat Insignia

Use of insignia devices on officers' hats varied as much as the hats themselves. Some forage caps have been noted with just the numeral identification of the particular regiment on the front of the cap, while others have the standard curled horn of the infantry branch of service. Some officers' forage caps near the end of the war appear to have had small metal corps badges affixed to the top of the cap, well forward near the front. An unusual hat or cap wreath in the form of interlocking shamrocks surrounding the regimental numerical designation has been seen on two caps in period photographs,[8] and at least one excavated stamped brass example is known, obviously unique to some Irish unit.

Officers' Overcoats

No photographs of officers wearing overcoats have been observed but one can assume that the standard officers' cloak coat with silk frogging or the enlisted mans' dismounted overcoat with or without officer rank designation were worn during the winter months.

Officers' Coats and Jackets

Frock coats, shell jackets and various non-regulation coats have been observed in period photographs, with frock coats definitely predominant. Standard double-breasted coats are noted on field grade officers, major and above, and single-breasted coats on company grade officers. A most unusual double-breasted, four-button, thigh length sack coat with black velvet collar has been observed in a photograph of a staff officer in the last year of the war

Officers' Rank Devices

Rank designating shoulder straps were worn as proscribed by regulations. It would seem that a number of officers privately purchased expensive triple-bordered, oversize shoulder straps with appropriate rank devices attached, since they are readily apparent in a number of officer photographs, while other officers wore standard size shoulder straps.

Officers' Corps Badges

Corps badges originated in June 1862 in General Kearny's division and were officially authorized by General Joseph Hooker in 1863.[9] They were very popular in the latter stages of the conflict and many Irish Brigade officers have been noted wearing private purchase metallic examples pinned high on the left breast of their uniform coats. The wearing of corps badges on headgear has already been mentioned.

Officers' Trousers

Field officers wore sky blue kersey trousers, and staff officers wore dark blue wool trousers with a narrow bullion stripe down the outseam.

Officers' Footwear

Officer's footwear appears to have been predominantly regulation or private purchase high boots worn inside trouser legs or with trouser legs tucked in to boot tops, at the whim of the individual. Some officers may have worn standard pattern Jefferson boots.

Officers' Side Arms and Accouterments

The great majority of officers appear to have utilized the regulation side arms and accouterments then in use, such as the Model 1851 sword belt with rectangular eagle sword belt plate, issue cap box and revolver holster, and revolver ammunition cartridge box. The make of revolver is not known but was most likely a Colt or Remington handgun. Period photographs indicate a preference for cavalry sabers[10] and non-

Above: *Colonel Henry Thomas Fowler, right, and another unidentified field grade officer, of the 63rd New York Volunteer Infantry, Irish Brigade. Both wear the double-breasted frock coat with two rows of seven buttons, and dark blue trousers.*

Below: *Excavated stamped brass hat wreath utilizing Irish shamrocks rather than the standard oak leaves. Similar insignia have been observed on the headgear of Irish officers.*

regulation European imported swords with metal scabbards, the latter probably a lesson learned from hard field duty with fragile leather sword scabbards and resultant damage to them.

Priests' Attire

Priests who served with the Irish Brigade wore modified officers' uniforms or civilian clothes of their choice. Father Corby told Professor James Edwards long after the war that he customarily wore a light cassock under his uniform that was "drawn up around the upper part of his body so that it could be easily lowered when on active duty as a priest." Apparently Corby could not remember if he had time to pull it out at Gettysburg, when he gave absolution to the brigade before it went into battle, but was certain he had put around his neck a purple stole that he always carried in his pocket.[11] Some photographs of Father Corby in the field show him in nondescript civilian attire. Reverend James Dillon, attached to 63rd New York Volunteers, was photographed in a dark coat with dark buttons, possibly civilian attire.

Enlisted Men's Headgear

The Pattern 1861 forage cap with regimental numerals affixed to the front was the headgear commonly worn by enlisted ranks of the brigade. A first sergeant of the 88th New York Volunteers is shown in a photograph wearing a low-crown chasseurs style forage cap with the numerals 88 on the front in the proscribed manner.[12] As the war continued, headgear was replaced as needed and pattern variations certainly occurred, but some form of forage cap remained part of the uniform throughout the war. Corps badges were worn appropriately on the crown of the cap upon authorization in 1863.

Enlisted Men's Overcoats

Enlisted ranks wore the regulation sky blue kersey overcoat for dismounted troops. This long coat had a cape attached that reached to the elbow. Mulholland in his memoirs notes that the 116th Pennsylvania drew overcoats on October 6, 1862, the same day as the regiment was ordered to Harpers Ferry and assigned to the Irish Brigade, and the whole brigade wore their overcoats in the assault on Marye's Heights at Fredericksburg in December 1862.

Enlisted Men's Coats

The three New York regiments of the Irish Brigade initially wore the New York State issue eight-button jacket with epaulets, collar, and belt loop piped in blue branch of service color. Non-commissioned officers' rank was indicated by regulation blue worsted wool chevrons of appropriate ranks on each sleeve between the shoulder and elbow. As the war progressed the soldiers of the brigade adopted the standard four blue wool sack coat authorized in 1859, although some enlisted ranks were photographed in frock coats

Enlisted Men's Trousers

All enlisted ranks wore the regulation sky blue kersey trousers so popular in the Union Army for the duration of the war.

Enlisted Men's Footwear

The Federal issue Jefferson boot was the standard footwear of the men of the Irish Brigade. These heavy, square-toed brogans were sturdy and serviceable but the incredible marches of the brigade constantly wore out shoes and there was a continual need for re-supply.

Top: *Lieutenant Colonel George W. Cartwright, 28th Massachusetts Volunteer Infantry. He wears the standard frock coat for field grade officers and has his slouch hat in his right hand with the II Corps badge prominently affixed to the side of the hat.*

Above: *Blue wool forage cap typical of those worn by soldiers of the Irish Brigade in 1863 until the end of the war. The red trefoil on the top indicates the wearer belongs to the 1st Division, II Corps. The stamped brass letter and numerals specify Company K, 63rd New York Volunteer Infantry.*

Enlisted Men's Accouterments

The Model 1858 Federal issue canteen with blue wool cover bearing white painted company letter and regimental numeral designation and white cotton cloth shoulder strap was standard equipment for the brigade. This canteen supplied by the Quartermaster Department was about seven-and-a-half inches in diameter and held some three pints of liquid. This was one piece of essential equipment that no soldier discarded.

The black-painted canvas haversack was another essential piece of equipment that was used to carry rations when issued of greasy bacon, hardtack and coffee. The body was about eleven by twelve inches and it had a shoulder strap that allowed it to be slung over the right shoulder to hang on the left hip under the canteen. The tin coffee cup carried by every soldier was usually secured to the haversack by the haversack closure tab.

The regulation Pattern 1839 brass oval US belt plate on the Pattern 1851 black bridle leather waist belt was used to carry a brass-tipped bayonet scabbard for the longarm in use, and a black leather cap box to hold caps necessary to fire the musket. A cartridge box, for either.69 caliber ammunition (Pattern 1839 or Pattern 1857) or .58 caliber ammunition (Pattern 1857 or 1861), was carried on a black bridle leather shoulder sling over the left shoulder, placing the box on the right hip The box had a brass oval US plate affixed to the flap and the shoulder belt had a circular eagle plate attached to the front.

Non-commissioned officers carried the same accouterments but wore a Pattern 1851 rectangular eagle plate on the waist belt and often carried a brass-hilted Model 1840 NCO sword in a special frog on the waist belt or shoulder belt.

Left: *Enlisted man of the 88th New York Volunteer Infantry in 1863, wearing the short state-issue shell jacket, white canvas gaiters and accouterments with a brass US belt plate.*

Above right: *Privately purchased from the regimental sutler or military store, stamped brass identity disks were the forerunner of the "dog tag."*

Knapsacks were carried on the march and contained spare clothing, such as an extra shirt, socks and underwear. One or two blankets with a large US woven in the center were also carried rolled on the top of the knapsack, often inside an India rubber blanket that Private McCarter of the 116th Pennsylvania often mentioned. The knapsack most often used was the Model 1853/1855 double-bag black canvas pattern. McCarter also said that knapsacks were usually left behind when going into action but he carried his blankets in a roll over his right shoulder at Fredericksburg.[13]

Enlisted Men's Longarms

Several different model and caliber shoulder arms were used by the various regiments that formed the Irish Brigade at different times during the Civil War, but all were single-shot, muzzle-loading percussion arms.

With the exception of Company K, Meagher's Zouaves, the 69th New York State Militia was armed with the U.S. Model 1842 percussion musket. This arm was a smoothbore .69 caliber musket that was already obsolescent but had served well in the Mexican War. The piece was sturdy, reliable and easy to maintain. The musket weighed just over nine pounds and was nearly five feet in length. A triangular socket bayonet with an 18-inch blade could be quickly attached to the end of the barrel and was carried in a bayonet scabbard on the waist belt when not affixed to the musket. The weapon could be fired three times a minute by a trained soldier but had an effective range of less than 100 yards. Ammunition used was a prepared paper cartridge with a choice of projectile, round ball, buck and ball or buckshot, that was issued in packs of ten cartridges with percussion caps and carried in the cartridge box.

Company K was raised separately and joined the 69th New York State Militia which had preceded them to the Washington Defenses. This company was armed with the Model 1816 Musket, .69 caliber, altered to percussion with a Remington tape primer lock and rifled and sighted at

Above: *Model 1858 Federal canteen with blue woolen cover, issued to a soldier in Company B, 69th New York Volunteer Infantry, as indicated by stenciled painted cover.*

Below: *Paper-wrapped pack of ten .69 caliber buck and ball cartridges with caps for the Model 1842 Musket carried by elements of the brigade*

Above: *Wood ordnance ammunition crate that contained 1,000 rounds, 100 packs, of buck and ball cartridges for the percussion musket, and from which ammunition was issued to soldiers in the field. Soldiers normally carried forty rounds, four packs of cartridges, in the cartridge box.*

Below: *U.S. Model 1842 Musket, .69 caliber smoothbore, the obsolescent longarm carried by four regiments of the Irish Brigade until the spring of 1864. Many Irish Brigade officers preferred this weapon because of its deadly effect in close combat.*

Bottom: *U.S. Model 1861 Rifle-musket, .58 caliber, standard arm of Federal forces during most of the war. It was used to rearm and refit the brigade in 1864. The reduced caliber, increased accuracy and greater range of the rifle-musket were greatly appreciated by the soldiers.*

the time of alteration. Remington also furnished a socket bayonet of slightly different configuration from the original Model 1816 bayonet with these alterations.[14] This weapon weighed nearly ten pounds but was about the same length without bayonet as the Model 1842. Being a rifled arm, it fired a cylindro-conoidal bullet, a large Minie ball, and had an effective range of several hundred yards.

When the 63rd, 69th and 88th New York Volunteers were organized as the nucleus of the Irish Brigade all three regiments were eventually armed with the U.S. Model 1842 percussion musket and there is some evidence that the officer cadre preferred these short-range weapons loaded with buck and ball cartridge. It has been suggested that during early organization some of the companies were armed with imported Prussian Model 1809/39 .71 and .72 caliber, brass-mounted, smoothbore muskets.[15] This was possible because New York City speculator John Hoey imported thousands in 1861 and they were certainly available.[16]

The 116th Pennsylvania Volunteers were also armed with the U.S. Model 1842 percussion musket that were issued to the regiment September 6, 1862, while in Washington.[17] The regiment carried this arm during most of its service. Colonel St. Clair Mulholland, later the regimental commander, was one of those officers who championed the big smoothbore with buck and ball cartridge as a lethal close combat shoulder arm.

By the last year of the war during the Overland Campaign and the siege of Petersburg it had become apparent that the .58 caliber rifle-musket was a vastly superior weapon for the kind of war that had

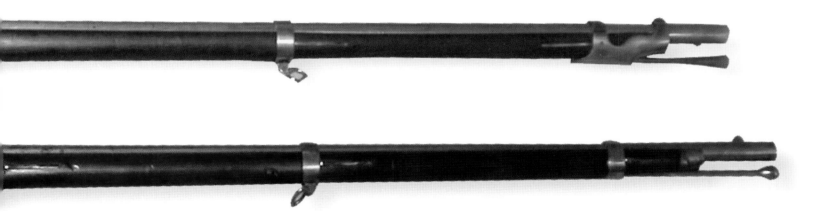

Above: *U.S. Model 1816 Musket, .69 caliber, altered to percussion and rifled and sighted at Frankford Arsenal in Philadelphia, using locks with the Maynard tape priming system supplied by the Remington Arms Company, Ilion, New York, in the mid-1850s. Twenty thousand obsolete 1816 longarms were upgraded using this alteration to extend the service life of the weapon. Captain Meagher's Zouave Company was the only company in the 69th New York State Militia armed with this type longarm at the Battle of First Bull Run. The arm is illustrated in the figure study of Company K on page 27.*

Below: *Regulation infantry regimental eagle drum of the 69th New York Volunteer Infantry. The regimental designation is painted on the riband above the eagle. William Hall and Company, a well-known musical instrument maker in New York City, manufactured this particular drum. Drums were essential to communicate orders in battle, and to provide music on the march.*

evolved. What was left of those regiments then comprising the Consolidated Brigade and then the reconstituted Irish Brigade were refitted and armed with the U.S. Model 1861 rifle-musket or derivative arm for the remainder of their service.

The 28th Massachusetts Volunteers were armed throughout their service with imported English Pattern 1853 rifle-muskets, .577 caliber, with triangular socket bayonets. These arms were purchased at the beginning of the war by Francis B. Crowninshield, agent for Governor James Andrew. The weapon weighed about nine pounds and was about five-and-a-half feet long. Effective range of the rifled weapon was three to five hundred yards, much greater than the smoothbore arms of the other regiments. This advantage evidently caused the Massachusetts soldiers extra hazardous duty since they were frequently assigned duties as brigade flankers or skirmishers.[18] Surviving examples have been noted with "28th Mass.," a company letter and soldier's number stamped on the tang of the brass buttplate, and at least one excavated specimen with a Fredericksburg provenance is known.[19] The English Pattern 1853 rifle-musket compared favorably with the U.S. Model 1861 rifle-musket with which the remainder of the regiment was eventually armed.

Irish Brigade Drum

Drums used in the brigade were the regular issue painted eagle drum. These drums usually were about sixteen inches in diameter and sixteen-and-a-half inches high. The retaining hoops were painted red, with the maple body painted blue and adorned with a great National eagle under a sun burst with a riband in its beak on which was lettered the regimental designation. William Hall & Son of New York City is known to have made an Eagle drum for the 69th New York Volunteers.[20]

Flags of the 69th New York State Militia and Irish Brigade

The first flag associated with the Irish Brigade is that of its predecessor unit, the 69th New York State Militia commanded by Colonel Michael Corcoran in 1860. In that year the regiment and Colonel Corcoran refused to parade and attend a reception for the visiting English Prince of Wales, Prince Albert Edward, later King Edward VII, because of deep-seated feelings for the

Above center: *Prussian Model 1803/1839 .71 caliber smoothbore musket. A few of these heavy, brass-mounted muskets may have been purchased by the 69th New York State Militia prior to reporting for duty in the Washington area. Rated as third class weapons, they were quickly replaced.*

Above: *English Pattern 1853 rifle-musket, .577 caliber. This imported longarm was equivalent to the U.S. Model 1861 rifle-musket and could use the same ammunition. The 28th Massachusetts was armed with the "Enfield rifle" supplied by the state, and carried them throughout the war.*

"A few days after our return to Bolivar Heights from Charles-town, the 116th Pennsylvania received a beautiful new silk regimental flag, heavily fringed with golden tinsel….each man there and then renewed his pledge and determination to 'Stand by that Flag,' the glorious emblem of his country's nationality, to the last or to perish beneath its folds."

William McCarter, a member of the 116th Pennsylvania Volunteers, in his book *My Life In The Irish Brigade.*

political situation in England and Ireland at that time. This embarrassing incident caused a political furor in the country but, at the same time, catapulted Colonel Corcoran to the stature of an Irish hero. One result was the presentation of a flag to the unit on March 16, 1861, by the grateful Irish citizens of New York commemorating the incident. The flag has been known ever since as the Prince of Wales Flag.

The rectangular, hand-embroidered color was five feet six inches on the staff and six feet eight inches on the fly. The one-sided flag had a field of green with red scrolls and gold lettering, sunburst design and fringe. The tassels and cords were also gold. The scroll above the sunburst read "PRESENTED TO THE 69TH REGIMENT" and the scroll below read "IN COMMEMORATION OF THE 11TH OCT. 1860". The scrolls and sunburst were embroidered as separate pieces and then sewn to the field as appliqués. There is no decoration on the reverse, only the outline of the obverse. This flag and a regimental National flag were the two flags carried by the 69th New York State Militia at the Battle of First Bull Run. The national flag was captured along with Colonel Corcoran, two officers and nine enlisted men.

When the regiment returned to New York City for muster out in 1861 the Prince of Wales flag and a national flag borrowed from the 7th Regiment New York State Militia led the parade. The Prince of Wales flag was carried in all parades and displayed at every function of the regiment in the city during the Civil War. It was paraded by the regiment in later years but never left the city for war again. The flag was restored once in the 1970s and resides presently in the 69th Regiment Armory in New York City.[21]

The Irish Brigade originally consisted of three regiments; the 63rd, 69th and 88th New York Volunteers. In compliance with regulations, each regiment was authorized a National flag and a regimental flag, and at least two flank guides. It appears that, during the war, these three regiments received four issues of colors. On November 7, 1861, a committee representing the Irish-American ladies and gentlemen of New York City presented a national flag and an Irish green color to the 63rd New York Volunteers. At about the same time other friends of the regiment gave the unit a regimental flag. These flags were the colors the regiment carried through all the battles until after Antietam in September 1862.

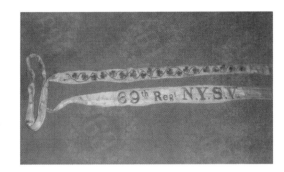

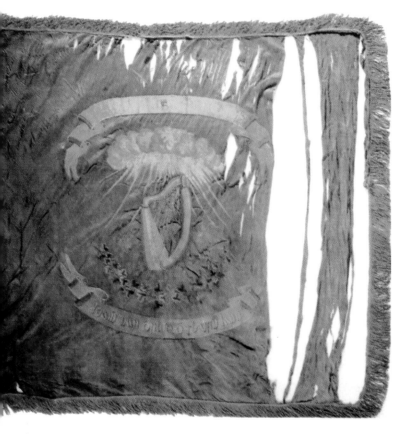

Above: *Green silk First Irish Colors presented to the 69th New York Volunteer Infantry in November 1861. This flag led the regiment at the Battle of Antietam and was retired and returned to the regimental armory in New York for safe keeping in November 1862.*

Opposite page: *Top, restored third green Irish flag of the 28th Massachusetts presented to Colonel Byrnes, May 5, 1864. Bottom, restored second green (Tiffany) Irish flag of the 28th Massachusetts. This flag led the Irish Brigade up Marye's Heights at Fredericksburg.*

The 69th and 88th New York Volunteers were given stands of flags, a national and Irish color, but of different pattern, by another group of Irish-American ladies of the city on November 5, 1861, and the two regiments carried those flags through the Battle of Antietam. In November 1862 a deputation of officers carried the tattered and torn first Irish colors to New York City for safekeeping and to secure replacements.

In December 1862 a group of thirty-four prominent New York Republican merchants presented all three regiments with fabulous silk national and Irish flags fabricated by Tiffany & Company. These flags are known as the Second (Tiffany) colors and cost the then enormous sum of $2,000.[22] Before these new flags could be delivered the brigade became combat ineffective after the suicidal assaults at Fredericksburg. The flags were received the day after the battle at a reception and feast held under hostile artillery fire in Fredericksburg. The flags were accepted but returned to New York for safekeeping until the brigade was back up to strength. Thus the Second (Tiffany) flags never saw battle. Coincidentally, at about the same time, December 1862, the City of New York presented all three regiments with another set of flags and these flags, known as the Third (New York City) flags, arrived in January 1863.

The brigade was little more than two battalions in actual strength after Fredericksburg. During the Battle of Gettysburg they probably carried the Third (New York City) National flag of the 63rd New York and the Third (New York City) Regimental of the 88th New York, but all references are ambiguous. Regardless, Irish green flags were never carried into battle by the units for the remainder of the war.

The three regiments were consolidated into a provisional regiment in 1864 and only one flag, the Third (New York City) National flag, was carried. In February 1865 another set of flags was authorized by the City of New York for the reconstituted Irish Brigade. Thus, the Fourth (1865 New York City) flags were issued at the close of the war, but it is not known if they were at General Lee's surrender at Appomattox.

The Second (Tiffany) Colors were reactivated and led the regiments of the Irish Brigade during the Grand Review in Washington, DC, May 23, 1865. These colors are also seen in photographs of Irish Brigade officers taken at the end of the war.[23]

The flags of the 116th Pennsylvania Volunteers were state issue from the Commonwealth of Pennsylvania. The national flag had the regimental designation on the center red stripe of the field. The regimental flag bore the Federal eagle surmounted by the national shield with unit designation on a red riband below it and an arc of stars above it. These

COLORS OF THE IRISH BRIGADE

"The ladies of New York had prepared their colors, to present to the regiment previous to their departure. The ceremony was a most inspiring one, and was attended by some of the most respectable and fashionable ladies and gentlemen of the city. The flags were six in number, with a corresponding number of guidons, and were of the richest silk, and executed in Tiffany's best style.

The national flags were magnificently embroidered, and fringed with saffron-colored silk; the stars were of white silk on a blue field, and in the center, in a crimson stripe, was the name of the regiment. The staffs were surmounted by a globe, with a gilt eagle, with the mounting heavily plated with gold and embellished with two rich crimson tassels pendent from each.

The regimental flags were of deep rich green, heavily fringed, having in the center a richly embroidered Irish harp, with a sunburst above it and a wreath of shamrock beneath. Underneath, on a crimson scroll, in Irish characters, was the motto, "They shall never retreat from the charge of lances." Each flag bore the numerical designation of its respective regiment; namely, Sixth-ninth Regiment New York State Volunteers, First Regiment Irish Brigade, Eighty-eighth and Sixty-third the same, but designated according to their respective numbers.

The staff-mountings were silver-plated; the top being a pike-head, under which was knotted a long bannerol of saffron-colored silk, fringed with bullion, and marked with the number of the regiment.

These flags looked gorgeous, and the needlework, performed by the fair donors themselves, was exquisitely executed. The guidons were got up with like taste and elegance, and had the State and brigade number of the regiments embroidered on each. The presentation took place at the residence of his Grace the Most Reverend Archbishop Hughes, in Madison Avenue, on the 18th November."

Captain David Power Conyngham,
The Irish Brigade and Its Campaigns.

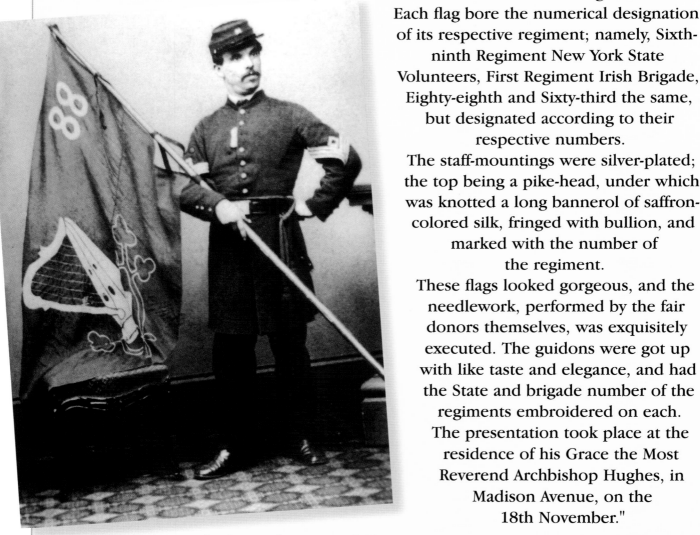

Above: *88th New York Volunteer Infantry sergeant holding a flank guide or marker emblazoned with Irish shamrock and harp.*

Above: *The second National (Tiffany) colors of the 69th New York Volunteer Infantry. The canton has the embroidered stars "in Tiffany's best style" and the 10th and 11th stripes have the unit designation and Irish Brigade embroidered thereon. Originally, this flag probably measured about six by six-and-a-half feet. The staff does not appear to be the one described in the presentation ceremonies. This historic flag resides today in the armory of the 69th New York National Guard in New York City.*

stands of flags were probably issued from the Philadelphia Depot throughout the war.

The flags of the 28th Massachusetts Volunteers were also different. This regiment had been assigned to the Irish Brigade in November 1862. General Meagher presented an Irish flag made by Tiffany & Company, similar to those already presented to the three New York regiments, to the new Massachusetts unit. The flag had a green silk field emblazoned with a golden harp and gold fringe. The red riband above the harp was lettered "4th Regiment Irish Brigade". The whole flag was completely embroidered by hand in the best Tiffany style. This flag of the 28th Massachusetts Volunteers was the only green flag to lead the Irish Brigade up Marye's Heights.

The regiment sent their battle-torn national flag home on December 26, 1862, and the state issued a replacement, their Second National flag, at the end of January. It was this second issue national flag and the Irish green Tiffany flag that the regiment carried in all engagements until the spring of 1864. Governor Andrew presented Colonel Richard Byrnes, commanding, with a Third National flag with a lighter blue canton and another state flag that had the state seal on a buff yellow field. This state flag was left at home and never carried in the field. It was this Third National flag that was carried in the Grand Review, May 23, 1865, The third green flag known as the Grainger flag was probably never carried in the field. Surviving Massachusetts flags are preserved in Boston.[24]

Above: *The second Irish (Tiffany) colors, now restored, reside in the archives of the University of Notre Dame in South Bend, Indiana.*

"I can promise you no more, than to assure you that (this flag) will be a fresh incentive to the brave men who are periling their lives in defense of that flag which typifies Union and liberty, and beneath which the shamrock has ever bloomed. In a few days, this flag will throw its emerald folds to the breeze, and the smoke of battle will encircle it; its freshness and beauty may be tarnished, but while there is an Irish arm to strike in its defense, its honor shall never, never be sullied or impaired. I can only point to the past history of my regiment to vouch for the future. Neither Massachusetts nor the historic fame of our race need blush for such a regiment."

Col. Richard Byrnes in a speech made in May 1864 upon receiving a new green regimental flag from citizens of Boston at the Parker House Hotel.

Chapter 3

The Formation of the Brigade

The genesis of the Irish Brigade may be traced back to the authorization of the 69th Regiment New York State Militia on November 1, 1851. This regiment was the sixty-ninth regiment state-wide to be accepted and only the second of predominant Irish stock. Michael Corcoran, an immigrant with prior military experience, became a proud private of Company I, the Irish Rifles. The militia system in New York was much the same as that in surrounding states. The men met frequently for drills and balls, and membership fostered military and social responsibilities. In a predominantly Irish unit like the 69th there was a volatile mix of Irish nationalism and American patriotism that was hard to separate. Thus, such a unit was a breeding ground and haven for all who would see Ireland free of English rule.[1]

It was no accident that this particular regiment provided an escort and attended a reception in May 1852 for the already internationally known Irish patriot and orator, Thomas Francis Meagher, when he arrived in New York after escaping from Tasmania. The English government had banished him there for life as (reduced) punishment for fomenting revolution in Ireland. Meagher had previously been sentenced to be hanged, drawn and quartered, a rather harsh and seemingly redundant punishment, but the sentence was mercifully commuted in 1849.[2] Corcoran and Meagher were cut from the same cloth, and the future of both men was intertwined.

The 69th New York State Militia performed the mundane part-time duties and drills typical for such organizations, and without incident until the unit was activated the summer of 1857 to deal with a raging yellow fever epidemic. The sickness was blamed on immigrants such as the Irish and all the sick were transported to a quarantine hospital on Staten Island. The 69th Regiment was sent over in October to relieve the American unit then guarding the facility. The unit being relieved detested the Irish 69th but the Irishmen accepted poor treatment with style and grace and performed the required duty in an exemplary manner. After fourteen days' service they were deactivated, to the accolades of senior officers in the brigade.[3]

By this time Michael Corcoran was obviously a rising star, having been elected captain of Company A. Popularity among the men and superior performance of duty was recognized when Corcoran was elected colonel of the regiment in August 1859.[4]

Below: *Furious action on Henry House Hill during the Battle of First Bull Run. The 69th New York State Militia and the 11th New York Fire Zouaves fight Confederate troops for possession of the "Prince of Wales" flag presented to the 69th NYSM at the same time Colonel Corcoran received his sword. A soldier from Company K, Meagher's Zouaves, can be seen in the right foreground.*

The following year, at the invitation of President James Buchanan, the Prince of Wales, Albert Edward, son of England's Queen Victoria, visited New York City in an official capacity. Almost in a state of hysterical adulation, the city government and New York society announced a parade and reception in his honor, to be held on October 11. The Irishmen of the of the 69th met and voted in true democratic militia style not to participate in the parade nor attend the reception, as a silent protest at what they felt was England's denigrating policy toward

Below: *Recruiting broadside of the 69th New York appealing to the patriotism of the Irish-American community and utilizing Irish antipathy toward England. Initially, Irishmen flocked in numbers to volunteer for service but as the casualty lists began to grow the harsh realities of war made recruitment difficult.*

Above: *Recruiting broadside of the 28th Massachusetts Volunteer Infantry, complete with Irish harp and shamrocks. The harp is flanked on either side by the battle cry of the regiment, "Faugh A Ballaugh" (Clear The Way).*

motherland Ireland. As colonel of the regiment Corcoran graciously accepted their decision and refused to issue the order for the unit to parade. His enemies, a vocal, socially prominent and powerful anti-Irish group, demanded his head on a platter.

In this politically charged atmosphere, Colonel Corcoran was arrested, charged, and ordered to stand court martial. All over the country his friends and admirers, Irish and non-Irish, went wild. In mid-March a huge gathering was held in the City Assembly Rooms on Broadway, at which time a beautiful presentation "sword of honor" was presented to Colonel Corcoran and a green silk flag was bestowed on the 69th Regiment. Both sword and flag were identically inscribed: "In commemoration of the 11th of October 1860," the day the colonel and his regiment refused to parade. To great applause, the flag was carried with pride by the regiment in the St. Patrick's Day parade, March 17, 1861. Corcoran also received a presentation gold-headed cane from South Carolina, a huge gold medal from California, and other honors.

The actual court was convened in early spring and the colonel behaved in the dignified manner of an officer and gentleman, until he fell ill and was put to bed. Then, at 4:30 in the morning on April 12, 1861, Confederate General P. G. T. Beauregard ordered the guns around Charleston Harbor to open fire on the Federal Fort Sumter, the first shots in a four-year Civil War that was to become the bloodiest ever in the southern hemisphere.

The 69th Regiment voted again, this time in favor of tendering its services for three months to the United States. All charges against the rebellious colonel were shortly thereafter dismissed. The Civil War had begun and there were more important duties for Colonel Corcoran and the 69th New York State Militia.

There was almost a stampede of volunteers to serve with the 69th, and several thousand were turned away.[5] The unit was ordered to Washington by Governor Edwin D. Morgan. Acrimony and bitterness against Colonel Corcoran and the 69th was forgotten in the cheering and flag waving that sent the regiment out of New York Harbor aboard the steamer *James Adger* on April 23, only eleven days after the first gun had sounded at Charleston. The regiment was presented a beautiful silk national flag on the way to the docks, and Corcoran, still so ill that he was forced to ride in a carriage, led his men to the wharf from which they embarked for Annapolis. The Irishmen were among the first troops to leave New York bound for the war.[6]

Above: *The 69th New York State Militia leaves New York for the war on April 23, 1861, only eleven days after the firing on Fort Sumter in Charleston Harbor. An Irish flag may be seen on the wagon with the patriotic drape proclaiming, "No North, No South," center foreground, and the parade is led by a zouave unit at the corner. Colonel Corcoran was still too ill to lead the regiment and had to be carried to the docks in a carriage. The regiment was presented a beautiful silk National flag at this time. The 69th was already carrying their "Prince of Wales" flag received earlier in March. The unit boarded the steamer James Adger that carried them to Annapolis, Maryland. Subsequently, the regiment went into garrison in the defenses surrounding Washington.*

Jumping into the patriotic frenzy sweeping the city, Thomas Francis Meagher announced on the same day his desire to raise a zouave company that would be attached to the 69th and serve under Colonel Corcoran. Meagher completed the organization of his company in only three days, during which he was forced to turn away hundreds of Irish volunteers. But bureaucracy kept him from joining the 69th as quickly as he would have liked.[7] By June, however, Meagher and his men had joined Corcoran in the capital but, rather than fighting, the regiment drilled and practiced the school of the soldier, and then drilled some more. When they couldn't drill any more the men were put to work building a huge earthwork defensive position on Arlington Heights, soon to be known as Fort Corcoran, one of the strongest fortifications in the defenses of Washington. Manual labor, the pick and shovel, were nothing new to the Irishmen, and they built the fort in an astonishingly short time, just one week, working around the clock despite the heat.[8]

Political pressure, both North and South, forced the opposing armies reluctantly into the field to do battle. Northern forces under the command of Brigadier General Irvin McDowell, who had absolutely no field command experience of any kind, left the defenses of Washington to probe in the direction of Manassas Junction, where Confederate forces

IRISH-MANNED UNITS THAT WERE NOT PART OF THE IRISH BRIGADE

Prewar militia units were part of the social fabric of the country and many men with martial spirit and political aspirations gravitated toward these organizations in the decades preceding the Civil War. Large numbers of Irish immigrants saw participation as an avenue to embrace their new country and facilitate assimilation as Americans at the same time. Many of these units adopted colorful names indicative of their country of origin or political alliance and those units that fought in the war on both sides were assigned official military designations upon muster into state and federal service. The following compilation is an incomplete list of Irish units, North and South, that were not affiliated with Meagher's Irish Brigade and presents original or local synonym names and then the official military designation. Many other additional units in both armies did not choose ethnic specific designations for various reasons. The total number of "Irish" units is much larger.

UNION

Irish Regiment (9th Connecticut Infantry)

Irish Brigade or James A. Mulligan's Brigade or 1st Irish Regiment (23rd Illinois Infantry)

Irish Legion (90th Illinois Infantry)

1st Irish Regiment (35th Indiana Infantry)

2nd Irish Regiment (61st Indiana Infantry, afterward part of 35th)

Patrick Naughton's Irish Dragoons (Company L, 5th Iowa Cavalry)

Faugh a Ballagh Regiment or 1st Irish Regiment (9th Massachusetts Infantry)

Andrew Mahony's Irish (Company E, 19th Massachusetts Infantry)

3rd Irish Regiment (55th Massachusetts Militia Infantry, part, later Companies G, H, I and K, 48th Massachusetts Militia Infantry for 9 months' service)

Stoughton Irish Guards (Company K, 9th Massachusetts Infantry)

Edward Doyle's Irish Regiment (27th Michigan Infantry, part)

Irish Regiment (10th New Hampshire Infantry)

Corcoran Zouaves (164th New York Infantry)

Corcoran's Irish Legion, 1st Regiment (182nd New York Infantry)

Corcoran's Irish Legion, 2nd, formerly 5th Regiment (155th New York Infantry)

Corcoran's Irish Legion, 3rd Regiment (164th New York Infantry)

Corcoran's Irish Legion, 4th, formerly 2nd Regiment (170th New York Infantry)

Corcoran's Irish Legion, 5th Regiment (Companies A, B and C, 175th New York Infantry)

Irish Rifles (37th New York Infantry

Hibernian Guards (Company B, 8th Ohio Infantry, three months)

Hibernian Target Company, (Company C, 2nd Pennsylvania Reserve Infantry)

Irish Dragoons, James A. Gallagher's Battalion (13th Pennsylvania Cavalry, part)

Irish Infantry, (Company F, 13th Pennsylvania Reserve Infantry)

Irish Regiment (24th Pennsylvania Infantry, three months)

Irish Regiment (69th Pennsylvania Infantry)

Irish Brigade (17th Wisconsin Infantry)

CONFEDERATE

Irish Battalion (1st Virginia Infantry Battalion, Provisional Army)

Irish Brigade, Company A (Company I, 6th Louisiana Infantry)

Irish Brigade, Company B (Company F, 6th Louisiana Infantry)

Irish Jasper Greens (Company A, 1st Georgia Volunteers)

Irish Volunteer Guards (a company of the 8th Georgia Infantry)

Irish Volunteers, Company A (Company D, 1st Georgia Volunteers)

Irish Volunteers, Company B (Company E, 1st Georgia Volunteers)

Irish Volunteers (Company F, 7th Louisiana Infantry)

Irish Volunteers (Company A, 1st Virginia Infantry Battalion, Provisional Army)

Irish Volunteers (Company C, 1st South Carolina Infantry Battalion)

Irish Volunteers (Company C, 19th Battalion Virginia Artillery)

under the command of Brigadier General Beauregard were reported to be concentrated. Colonel William Tecumseh Sherman, who later became one of the ranking northern generals, commanded the 3rd Brigade of the 1st Division, to which Colonel Corcoran and the 69th New York State Militia were assigned. According to Athearn, Corcoran received orders on July 15 to move the following day and ordered "blankets to be rolled up close and slung over the left shoulder under the right arm – muskets were to be in the best order – cartridge boxes full – each man to carry three days' rations in his haversack."[9]

Following hours of delay, the Union forces finally got under way during the afternoon of July 16 and, after several days of marching with intermittent alarms caused by the proximity of Confederate forces, arrived at Centreville, Virginia, some twenty miles southwest of the capital. General McDowell's plan was to flank the Confederate forces deployed west of winding Bull Run, a creek near Manassas Junction at the intersection of the Warrenton Turnpike and the Manassas-Sudley Road, at Sudley Springs.

The Union force of about 43,000 men went into motion early the morning of July 21, but there was considerable confusion among them. The flanking force was three hours late crossing Sudley Springs and Confederate forces were there to contest the movement, but by noon had been forced back into a defensive position around Henry House Hill just south of the Warrenton Turnpike. Union forces had crossed the stone bridge over Bull Run and by mid-day had established contact with the Union flanking forces coming down from Sudley Springs.

Above: *A stone bridge on the Warrenton Turnpike near Bull Run. This strategic span became a major bottleneck in the precipitous retrograde movement of the Federal army in their frantic efforts to leave the Bull Run battlefield and return to the safety and security of the Washington defenses. As the disorganized Federal troops raced back toward Centreville, Confederate artillery hit a wagon on the bridge over Cub Run. Colonel Corcoran had already been separated from the regiment and captured by Confederate mounted elements. Acting Major Meagher, already wounded and carried from the field, was thrown from a wagon into a creek, possibly near here, while trying to leave the battle area. The 69th NYSM lost its colonel and nearly 200 men were killed or captured in this first clash of amateur armies. Survivors reached Washington early the next morning.*

Opposite page: *19th century Currier and Ives lithograph depicting Colonel Corcoran, mounted on white horse, leading the 69th NYSM, with the green Irish flag, inaccurately illustrated, and National color in the background, at the Battle of Bull Run, July 21, 1861. Soldiers in the foreground wearing white havelocks and red shirts are the 11th New York Fire Zouaves. The two regiments were intermingled during the confused assaults on Henry House Hill. The incident depicted in the illustration on page 41 probably occurred around this time, and the action is shown there much more accurately.*

Sherman's Brigade had been held in reserve all morning but in early afternoon was called upon to come to the relief of Federal troops who had failed repeatedly to push Confederate forces away from the Henry House. Taking advantage of the defilade at the base of the hill, Sherman formed his line of battle, with the 13th New York acting as skirmishers and the 2nd Wisconsin first in line, followed by the 79th New York and with the 69th New York bringing up the rear.

The 2nd Wisconsin made two assaults and was repulsed with heavy losses. The 79th New York made one assault and was decimated. The men of the 69th dropped their knapsacks and overcoats and began the assault with a color bearer carrying the green Prince of Wales flag and with Colonel Corcoran and Acting Major Meagher mounted, leading the regiment. Artillery and small arms fire from General Thomas J. Jackson's five Virginia regiments was intense. The colonel was hit in the leg, and Meagher's horse was killed beneath him. But Meagher got to his feet, waving his sword and urging the men forward. Two color bearers of the green flag were shot down in short order.

The Irishmen made four heroic but unsuccessful attempts to break the Virginians' line. Finally, Colonel Sherman ordered the regiments to fall back and regroup in the original position. The wounded Corcoran managed to form a regimental square and lead the battered remains of the units off the field and onto the Turnpike. At this point, as they were re-crossing Bull Run, Sherman somehow gave the order to disperse for fear of Confederate cavalry cutting them off. All order was lost. In the confusion of retreat, Colonel Corcoran became separated from the regiment and was captured with a few men and the national colors by elements of the 13th Virginia Cavalry. On foot, Meagher climbed onto a wagon but, in the panic to cross the creek, the wagon overturned, throwing him into the water.[10]

The general panic worsened as the Union army streamed in disarray toward Centreville and on to Washington. The Irish 69th was swept up in this retreat. Meagher struggled out of the water and joined the mob of fleeing soldiers who eventually reached Fort Corcoran at 3:00 AM the morning of July 22 – tired, wet and hungry, and without their arms and equipment which lay scattered in the fields and along the retreat route. Ironically, because its three-month enlistment had expired on July 20, the regiment didn't really have to fight at Bull Run. The Irishmen had stayed because they thought it was the right thing to do.

Almost immediately fingers were pointed, assigning blame for the debacle at Bull Run. Unquestionably, Irvin McDowell was at fault, but so were others. Conflicting stories appeared in the New York *Daily Tribune* concerning Meagher's conduct. One piece had him "disgracefully running away from the battle." The same newspaper categorically denied the story the next day, but damage was done and Meagher was shaken

Above: *The ruins of the Henry House. The battle raged around this site most of the afternoon. The house was subjected to intense artillery and small arms fire even though it was not an objective. It was just unfortunately there....*

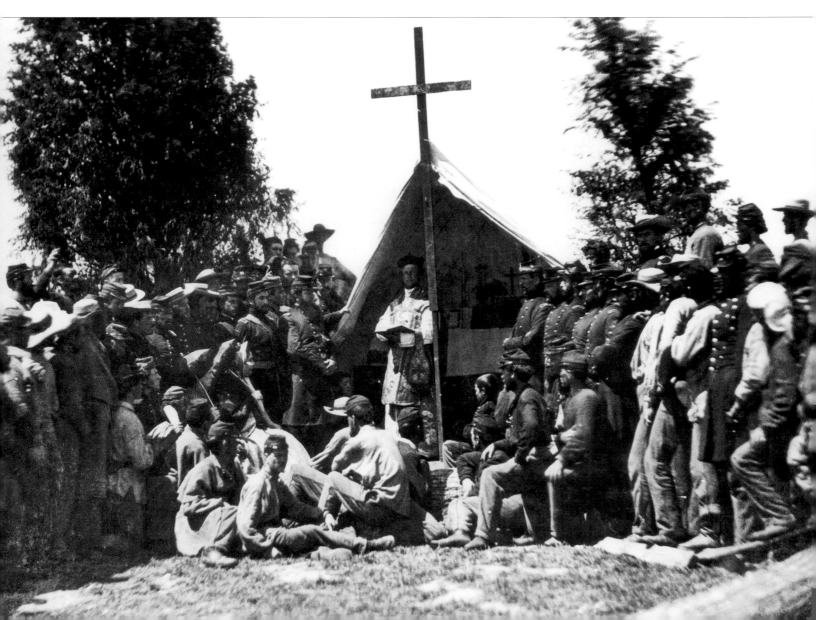

Above: *Regulation U.S. Model 1850 Staff and Field Officer's sword with brass-mounted steel scabbard, carried by Brigadier General Thomas Francis Meagher. The standard guard has the letters US rather than the harp noted in the Corcoran sword.*

and totally demoralized. Most importantly, Colonel Corcoran was gone and the men of the 69th Regiment were without a charismatic leader.

On Saturday July 27, after stops in Baltimore and Philadelphia, the exhausted regiment arrived at the Battery in New York and was greeted by a sixty-nine gun salute. The 7th Regiment loaned a national color and the 69th, led by Captain James Kelly, marched up Broadway to its armory on Essex Street, where the men were dismissed and told to report back and be mustered out on August 3, 1861.[11]

With Colonel Corcoran a prisoner of war, a power struggle for command of the regiment began as soon as it arrived home. Major James Bagley, who was also an alderman, wanted the command but had even

Above: *The center obverse portion of General Meagher's blade showing the etched letters US. The reverse bears the Federal eagle and other military motifs. The upper mount of the scabbard is somewhat crudely scratched "Maj. Gen. T. F. Meagher" completely encircling the mount – puzzling, since he never achieved that rank. The imported sword is otherwise unmarked except for "Iron Proof" etched on the back of the blade at the hilt, and it was probably made in Soligen, Germany. General Meagher's sword is at the University of Notre Dame.*

Left: *The strong influence of the Catholic Church over many members of Irish units cannot be underestimated. Those regiments to which priests were attached regularly observed mass in the field and even sometimes on the march. Instances of absolution before battle were not unusual. This rude "cathedral in the field" boasts an altar within the tent and a tall cross . Father Thomas H. Mooney, in full vestments, is leading the mass, attended by officers and men of the 69th New York State Militia, around Fort Corcoran, Arlington Heights, in the Washington defenses. Colonel Corcoran is standing with arms folded on the right nearest the tent. Some priests were unable to withstand the rigors of hard campaigns and their presence in the field dwindled as the war progressed. This was not the case with the Irish Brigade.*

less experience than Captain Meagher In the meantime, on the night of August 21, the regiment again voted to enlist for "the war" and its designation was changed to the 69th New York Volunteers, to be commanded by Lieutenant Colonel Robert Nugent with Meagher as a company grade officer.[12] Captain Meagher was offered several opportunities and higher rank with other regiments, and staff appointments, but heard of the rumor of the formation of a five-thousand-man Irish Brigade and bided his time. By late August the idea had developed into a reality. The command of the brigade was offered to General James Shields, an Irish veteran of the Mexican War, already 51 years old.[13]

On August 30, it was Captain Meagher and not Lieutenant Colonel Nugent who offered the services of the newly formed 69th New York Volunteers directly to President Lincoln. Meagher later denied this.[14] Nevertheless, Thomas A. Scott, Assistant Secretary of War, responded directly to Captain Meagher, addressing him as "Colonel" even though he was two ranks junior. Meagher was already renowned for his ignorance of the chain of command. Organization of the brigade was approved by September 7, 1861, with three New York regiments, and one each from Pennsylvania and Massachusetts. Shortly thereafter Colonel Meagher began recruiting in New York. Lieutenant Colonel Nugent recruited in Philadelphia. Meagher's old friend, B. S. Treanor, recruited for the unit in Boston. The veterans of the old 69th New York State Militia would form the cadre of the Irish Brigade.[15]

Colonel Meagher, again ignoring the chain of command, wired Secretary of War Simon Cameron that an Irish Brigade of five thousand men was ready to be accepted for Federal service. In early October anonymous sources spread rumors of General Shields' poor health. Shields was still on the West Coast in mid-October and stated that, while he was flattered with the offer of a brigade, he was already a brigadier general and hoped for a commission as a major general in the regular army. This was not forthcoming, and he served with mediocre success, resigning from the army in 1863.[16]

Meagher's skillful manipulation had adroitly pushed General Shields out of the picture. Colonel Meagher eagerly signed his first order as "Acting Brigadier" on October 21, 1861, ordering all officers to report to

Above: *Colonel Meagher, commanding officer of the 69th New York Volunteer Infantry (photographed at the same time as on page 14), wearing deluxe oversize shoulder straps favored by some officers of the brigade.*

Above: *Brigadier General James Shields, Irish Brigade commander apparent, until the wily Meagher maneuvered him out of the command.*

Following pages: *During the savage assaults by Confederate forces under General Jackson at Gaines' Mill, the 9th Massachusetts Volunteer Infantry, Colonel Thomas Cass commanding, refused to withdraw and was in danger of being overrun. In the nick of time, General Meagher, in one of his more elaborate uniforms – green velvet, topped off by a straw hat with green plume – led the 63rd New York to support the 9th and save the day.*

him at Fort Schuyler, New York, on the 25th, although his appointment had not yet been approved in Washington.

On November 7 a stand of flags was presented to the 63rd New York.[17] The other two New York regiments were presented with their flags, prepared by the ladies of the city, in front of Archbishop Hughes' residence on Madison Avenue on November 18. It was a very elaborate ceremony witnessed by a considerable crowd of the most influential and important people of the city.[18] The 69th left the city for Washington, and it eventually encamped at nearby Alexandria, Virginia, to be joined by the end of the month by the 63rd and 88th New York.

All the while, Irish political interests were in play lobbying for the appointment of Meagher as a brigadier, and a deputation of influential people called on President Lincoln. Meagher got the unofficial news of his appointment on December 27 and the Senate duly confirmed this by unanimous vote on February 3, 1862.[19] The new brigadier general formally assumed command of the Irish Brigade two days later and staged a grand review of the regiments, ironically accompanied by poor

Below: *The van of the 28th Massachusetts Volunteer Infantry, all wearing the dismounted infantry sky blue kersey overcoat, crosses one of the pontoon bridges on the Rappahannock River into the battered town of Fredericksburg on December 12, 1862. They are led by their color guard with the Second (Tiffany) Irish Color and National color. The occupation of the town came after weeks of numbing procrastination by General Ambrose E. Burnside, the Union commander, as the Army of Northern Virginia, led by General Robert E. Lee, daily strengthened fortifications that Federal forces would eventually have to face. Brigadier General Meagher, in forage cap, salutes. By his side is Major General Winfield Scott Hancock, his immediate superior, commanding the 1st Division, II Corps. The next day these flags would lead the brigade to everlasting fame and glory in one of the most futile assaults in recorded history.*

General Shields, and a rather large staff and many guests who later enjoyed a sumptuous banquet accompanied by appropriate libations. This elaborate social occasion evidently established a precedent for entertainment for which the Irish Brigade became well known throughout the Army of the Potomac for the rest of the war.[20]

On February 8, 1862, Brigadier General Meagher and the Irish Brigade were assigned to the division of Brigadier General Charles Vose Sumner at Alexandria, and reported to Camp California where the division spent the next few weeks in intensive training. The following month the division marched to Warrenton Junction in a frustrated attempt to outflank the Confederate forces there, and then returned to Alexandria in early April. Major General George Brinton McClellan, now in command, had decided on his Peninsula Campaign against Richmond and transported the new Army of the Potomac to the York Peninsula. The Irish Brigade sailed on the *Columbia* and the *Ocean Queen* to Fort Monroe, Virginia.[21] The real war was about to begin in earnest.

Chapter 4

The Making of the Legend

By mid-March 1862 General McClellan had gathered the largest, most thoroughly trained and best equipped army ever assembled on the North American continent. He then crammed it into four hundred vessels of every imaginable description on the Potomac River below Washington, in preparation for transporting this force to Fort Monroe at the tip of the Peninsula between the James and York Rivers. From there "Little Mac," as his men affectionately called him, planned to move up this finger between the two rivers to Richmond, just 100 miles away, assault and capture the Confederate capital, and end the war. To accomplish this goal he had an army of over 100,000 men, 25,000 horses, 300 pieces of artillery, 3,600 wagons, and 700 ambulances, and was urged by increasingly strident calls from President Lincoln and the Congress to get on with it.[1] The actual movement took several weeks but by the first week in April the army was on the Peninsula, for better or worse.

The men of the Irish Brigade made the trip in rough weather. Many were seasick and ill. On their arrival at Ship Point the weather was so bad that the men were unable to disembark for four or five days, and were confined to the rolling, dancing ships while a sleet-storm blanketed the area. When the men finally set foot on land the area was a sea of red Virginia mud. Brigade officers had made no plans for the shelter or feeding of the men on arrival, but fortuitously Howard's Brigade had preceded them and found shelter in an abandoned Confederate camp and his soldiers shared what shelter and rations they had with the cold, wet, hungry, and tired Irishmen. The next few days were filled unloading stores and equipment in the continuing rain, which did nothing to improve the morale of the men.[2]

At this time the Confederate lines, manned by only 12,000 men under General John B. Magruder, stretched across the Peninsula at Yorktown, just a scant seven miles up the narrow strip of land, but separated from the Union positions by low, swampy ground. Because of the appalling weather, the few narrow roads through the bogs had become impassable and required improvement before the army could even begin to move. So the Irish Brigade started off the campaign with the backbreaking labor of corduroying the roads, just so that the Federal forces could approach the Confederate entrenchments. At the end of the month the brigade was held in reserve at Camp Winfield Scott. The men were finally issued shelter halves that could be joined together to make tents, their first real shelter since arriving in the area.

Confederate forces quietly evacuated their Yorktown line on May 4 after the Federal army had spent weeks digging elaborate siege fortifications. During the month of May the Union army continued its snail's pace advance up the Peninsula toward the Confederate capital until it reached the Chickahominy River within sight of the church spires of Richmond. General McClellan split his forces, with three corps on the north side of the river and two corps remaining on the south side, less than six miles from the city.[3] Confederate General Joseph E. Johnston saw McClellan's division of forces as an opportunity to destroy the Union army piecemeal, and attacked at Seven Pines on May 31.

This was the same day that General Meagher, in an effort to boost sagging morale in his bedraggled command, chose to hold the Chickahominy Steeple-Chase, a day of fun and frolic, highlighted by two horse races and one mule race. First prize was a tiger skin to be presented by the general. A theater had been built to stage a play for the evening entertainment, and the party was well underway when the sound of artillery caused the merry event to be abruptly curtailed and the Irish Brigade to move to the sound of the guns.[4] The brigade's three regiments headed toward Seven Pines, marching most of the

Above: *The 63rd New York Volunteer Infantry drill in the field. Four regimental officers in the right foreground observe the evolutions. The regimental band is playing between the officers and the regiment drilling by companies.*

Below: *A Currier and Ives lithograph depicting Brigadier General T. F. Meagher at the Battle of (Fair Oaks) Seven Pines, Virginia, June 1, 1862, during General McClellan's ill fated Peninsula Campaign. Federal losses unnerved the already skittish McClellan and General Robert E. Lee assumed command of Confederate forces.*

night in pouring rain on unfamiliar roads through swamps and swollen creeks, and finally bivouacking for a few hours.

The next day, upon reaching the approaches to Grapevine Bridge on the Chickahominy, they found artillery bogged down to the hubs of the wheels. The men of the 63rd New York were detailed to assist the artillerymen in getting the guns moving. The 69th and 88th New York meanwhile crossed the rain-swollen river on the rickety bridge, against the advice of engineers, and hurried to support Union troops of General Darius Couch's division then under attack by Confederate columns. By late afternoon both regiments advanced to the edge of woods near the Adams House in support of Howard's Brigade that had preceded them. Here the two Irish regiments found themselves on the flank of the attacking Confederates and were able to assist in halting the Confederate advance.[5] While engaged, the two regiments, the 69th under Colonel Robert Nugent and the 88th under Patrick Kelly, played a supporting role and suffered a total of about 100 casualties.[6] As darkness approached, the firing stopped and the opposing forces retired to their previous positions, with little accomplished.

During the second day of the battle, toward evening, Confederate General Johnston was severely wounded. The following day General Robert E. Lee took command and the scattered Confederate armies and

> "A large body of infantry advance around our right and take up position in an open field. While we were wondering what troops they were, a breeze blew open the folds of a flag and we saw the green flag of Ireland. Then we knew it was Meagher's fighting Irish brigade, and we felt that not a man in that brigade would yield while life lasted, and where that green flag would lead it would be followed by every true son of Erin, even into the very jaws of death."
>
> From the regimental history of the 63rd Pennsylvania, 1st Division, III Corps, Army of the Potomac, which was in retreat from the Peninsula, March 1862

those units just arriving were united to form the Army of Northern Virginia. This change in command would have an enormous effect on the conduct of the war. For the next three weeks both armies consolidated positions. General Lee earned the appellation "King of Spades" for the amount of digging accomplished by the new Army of Northern Virginia, but the result of the labor was a well fortified city able to withstand whatever effort McClellan might make against it.

During this period, from June 12 to June 16, twelve hundred Confederate cavalry under the command of Brigadire General J. E. B. Stuart rode north from Richmond to the North Anna River. The next day the force swung eastward toward Hanover Court House and McClellan's exposed flank. Stuart encountered almost no resistance as he passed through Haw's Shop but did have a sharp fight with Federal troopers that were commanded, ironically, by his father-in-law, Brigadier General Philip St. George Cooke who was absent at the time. During this small engagement the Confederate cavalry suffered the one and only casualty of the entire raid.

Stuart had completed his mission by discovering that McClellan's right flank was in the air, not anchored on any defendable terrain feature, and therefore susceptible to flank attack. Rather than ride back the way he had come and encounter Federals who now knew he was on the loose, Stuart and his men rode on to Tunstall's Station and then over the Chickahominy River at Forge Bridge. Stuart, followed by his command, arrived back in Richmond to a hero's welcome, having ridden 100 miles around the whole Union Army.

Above: *Major General George Brinton McClellan, second in the West Point class of 1846, became major general of Ohio Volunteers, and rose to become general-in-chief of the armies, all in 1861.*

Below: *The 88th New York Volunteers, Colonel Patrick Kelly commanding, and the 69th New York Volunteers, Colonel Robert Nugent commanding, cross the Richmond and York Railroad to assault Confederate positions in the tree line east of (Fair Oaks) Seven Pines.*

George McClellan now knew positively that his supply base at West Point on the Pamunkey River was not secure, something that had bothered him for some time, and his natural caution was reinforced. He decided he had to move his supply base south to Harrison's Landing, where the Union Navy could protect and support his operations.

While Stuart was riding around the Union army the Irish Brigade was on the picket line in front the division positions. On June 9 the 29th Massachusetts Volunteers under Colonel Ebenezer Pierce was attached to the Irish Brigade, increasing the unit strength to four regiments. While the men were not Irish the manpower was welcome. The brigade was then part of the division under General Israel Bush Richardson, known as "Greasy Dick," who was absolutely fearless in battle. Richardson had assumed the command when old General Sumner was reassigned to corps command.[7]

Toward the end of June General Lee, expecting reinforcements from General Thomas J. Jackson coming from the Valley, and suspecting McClellan's imminent change of supply bases, probed the right Federal flank to the north of Richmond. On the June 26 the Confederates launched an assault against Fitz-John Porter's Fifth Corps stretched from Grapevine Bridge north to Meadow Bridge near Mechanicsville. Lack of coordination and an overly complicated battle plan doomed the action to failure. Lee's army suffered 1,500 casualties, losses in officers it could not afford, and achieved nothing.[8] Porter gathered his artillery and wagons and withdrew his corps in the direction of Gaines' Mill. His rear guard sporadically skirmished with advancing elements of Gregg's Brigade, the 1st and 12th South Carolina.

Elements of this rear guard were from Brigadier General Charles Griffin's 2nd Brigade, 1st Division, V Corps. By mid-afternoon Federal forces were being overwhelmed. Among Griffin's regiments the hardest hit was the Irish 9th Massachusetts Volunteers, Colonel Thomas Cass commanding. Seeing the green standard of the Irishmen, Jackson allegedly growled that his men should sweep away "that damned brigade."[9] The 9th Massachusetts doggedly refused to retreat and held its position in spite of heavy losses.

McClellan threw his last remaining reserves, Meagher's and French's brigades, into the fight. When it seemed Jackson's gray-clad troops were about to overrun the dwindling Irishmen, the Irish Brigade, the 63rd New York in advance with its green flag flying and General Meagher at the front, followed by the rest of the brigade, came to support the men of the 9th and stopped the Confederate assault.[10] The brigade maintained its defensive position all night while the baggage trains of the retreating army crossed the river to safety.

Meagher's brigade was ordered to report to McClellan's headquarters at Savage Station on the 28th, leaving the 69th New York to man the picket line of Sumner's rear guard. The four regiments were reunited the next day at Meadow Station and subsequently the brigade charged a

Above: *Brigadier General J. E. B. Stuart led elements of Confederate cavalry completely around General McClellan's army, June 12 to June 16, so alarming the Federal commander that he changed his base of supply from West Point south to Harrison's Landing on the James River.*

Below: *The Battle of Malvern Hill was the last engagement of the Peninsula Campaign, after which General McClellan's base of supply was secure at Harrison's Landing, protected by the Navy's guns. The Irish Brigade's Father William Corby, seated right, and Father James Dillon, seated center, are photographed with three unidentified comrades at this huge base.*

> "The Eighty-eighth in a moment dashes in with the Sixty-ninth, under a fierce fire from the enemy, who are concealed in the woods and a neighboring house; still, there is no faltering, but wild cheers, and on they press for the hill-top, where a hand-to-hand fight ensues. Men brain and bayonet each other. The enemy makes a bold stand to hold the hill, but in vain. They sullenly retire, but the darkness prevents our brave fellows from following them up. They send a parting good-night after them. Malvern Hill is fought. McClellan's army is saved, but that hillside is covered with the dying and the dead of the Irish Brigade."
>
> Captain David Powers Conyngham describing the Battle of Malvern Hill, July 1, 1862, in *The Irish Brigade and Its Campaigns.*

Virginia battery which it overran, capturing two guns that were disabled on the spot.[11] After dark the brigade was ordered to beat a retreat beyond White Oak Swamp. All army supplies were burned and Union dead and wounded were left behind at Savage Station.

The brigade marched all night to Nelson's Farm and, after destroying the bridge at that point, rested for some time before going into action again on June 30. During this time General Meagher was seen riding a gray horse conspicuously up and down the firing line under heavy small arms fire and declined to dismount when requested to do so. The general and his staff, gloriously decked out with ostentatious gold insignia, were easily seen and always attracted heavy Confederate fire when the mounted group were on the field of battle.[12]

At 1:00 AM on July 1 the brigade was again on the march south to Malvern Hill, which it reached at around 5:00 AM. After resting all day the men were in the midst of preparing supper when elements of the 69th and 88th New York were ordered into position behind Berdan's Sharpshooters who manned the picket line. The 63rd New York and 29th Massachusetts were detailed to support some batteries and were not engaged in the fighting.

The Confederate attacks were vicious and sustained, with periods of close combat and bayonet charges. General Meagher was mounted throughout the fight, conspicuously encouraging his men. After dark, around 9:00 PM, the Confederate assaults on Malvern Hill ceased. After a few hours of rest the brigade and the army retreated again to Harrison's Landing, and to safety under the guns of the Union Navy. The retreat

Above: *Brigadier General T. F. Meagher with Colonel Robert Nugent, 69th New York Volunteer Infantry. Meagher resigned his commission in May 1863 after Chancellorsville and returned home to New York "to await orders." This image was probably taken on one of his periodic visits to the Irish Brigade. The general appears in civilian clothes but wears his favored Baldric box and holds a forage cap with general's insignia. He also wears a sash, sword belt and sword. The sword with large acorn sword knot is not the Model 1850 Staff and Field sword shown previously. Colonel Nugent also holds an interesting forage cap with what appears to be a feather affixed to it. Robert Nugent commanded the Irish Brigade on several occasions and at the end of the war*

route of the last week was littered with arms, accouterments, camp equipment and provisions, some abandoned, some destroyed. But as far as the men of the Army of the Potomac were concerned, "Little Mac" had conducted a successful campaign.

McClellan's retrograde movements during the Seven Days' had kept his army basically intact and moved his base of operations south to Harrison's Landing on the James River. Confederate forces under General Robert E. Lee had frustrated every move against Richmond and the Confederate capital was safe. Both armies had suffered major losses in personnel. Lee's army lost just over 20,000 men, some 25percent of his command. McClellan lost slightly fewer, about 16,000.[13] Nearly 500 of these casualties were from the three regiments of the Irish Brigade

The Union army rested at the vast depot at Harrison's Landing, and rearmed and refitted in early July. Because losses during the Seven Days' battles had drastically reduced ranks of the Irish Brigade, General Meagher requested leave to go to New York to recruit replacements. McClellan granted his request and the general departed on July 16. The monotony of camp life was broken on July 22 by a review of General Sumner's Corps, followed by a Grand Review of the whole army attended by President Lincoln.[14]

The Irish Brigade was on picket duty in the vicinity of Malvern Hill from early to mid-August, when General Meagher rejoined them.. His effort to recruit additional men for the brigade was almost a total failure. The reality of the war had greatly affected patriotism within the Irish community in the north.[15] On August 16 the brigade marched out of Harrison's Landing for Newport News to embark by ship for Acquia Creek, Virginia, to report for duty to General Burnside at Falmouth, Virginia. Subsequently, the brigade was marched back to Alexandria and then placed under the command of "Greasy Dick" Richardson – which greatly pleased the men – and were told to report to General Pope near Centreville.

While McClellan was floundering in the swamps of the Peninsula, Major General John Pope, one of the West Point Class of 1842 that produced seventeen general officers, was given command of all troops not under McClellan on the Peninsula, effective June 26. Pope's force was the Army of Virginia, with the mission of protecting Washington. General Pope was soundly beaten by General Lee and his Army of Northern

Opposite page, top: *Major General Israel Bush Richardson, known as "Fighting Dick" commanded the 1st Division, II Corps, at the Battle of Antietam, September 17, 1862. The Irish Brigade served in his division, and this fearless general commanded the respect of the wild Irishmen. Richardson led his division, with the Irish Brigade in the fore, into cornfield on the Roulette Farm by mid-morning. They charged the Confederate forces in the Sunken Road (Bloody Lane) but were eventually forced to retire after sustaining staggering losses and expending all ammunition. Later in the day General Richardson was mortally wounded by a shell fragment. A physically strong man, he lingered painfully for days and finally died November 3, 1862.*

Below: *View of the Plains of Manassas from the rough log cabin that was the headquarters of General T. F. Meagher. The tracks of the Orange and Alexandria Railroad run through the center of the image. Across the tracks are the neatly laid out camps of Brigadier General Richardson's Division. The rendering was done by "special artist" Edwin Forbes for Frank Leslie's Illustrated Newspaper, April 6, 1862.*

Virginia at the Battle of Second Bull Run on August 29 and 30, 1862, while the Irish Brigade was enroute to join his army. Meagher's Irishmen were not directly engaged in the battle, but assisted in a supporting role by covering General Pope's ignominious retreat back to Washington on August 31. Pope was immediately sent to the Department of the Northwest where he could do no further harm, and George McClellan was restored to full command of Union forces in Virginia on September 2, to the delight of all the men.

The Battle of Second Bull Run was a signal southern victory that left Union forces ever more confused and demoralized. General Lee seized the opportunity to take the Army of Northern Virginia into Maryland to threaten Washington and bring the horrors of war home to the northern population. Lee began his move north on September 5, assuming that his old antagonist, George McClellan, now back in charge of Union forces, would be as slow and cautious to move as he had been on the Peninsula. This was not the case, and Union forces caught up with elements of the Confederate army at South Mountain and a fierce battle took place between Lee's rear guard and advancing Federal troops.

Because of a confusing change in orders, Meagher and his Irish Brigade were not engaged at South Mountain on September 14. However, they did participate in the pursuit of those Confederate forces that fell back through Boonsboro, and established a strong defensive line on the west side of Antietam Creek before the small town of Sharpsburg, to await the arrival of other Confederate forces scattered between there and Harpers Ferry.

Why McClellan did not attack immediately on September 15, while Confederate forces were still scattered over the Maryland countryside, is yet another example of lost opportunities that plagued "Little Mac." His available forces greatly outnumbered those southern forces confronting him, but he procrastinated as usual while the Confederates concentrated and grew stronger by the hour. After some skirmishing during the afternoon and evening of September 16, Union forces began their assault about 5:30 AM, September 17, north of Sharpsburg.

The battle raged through the early morning while II Corps, with "Greasy Dick" Richardson's division and Meagher's brigade, were held in reserve on the east side of Antietam Creek. About 9:30 AM Richardson was ordered to ford the creek with his division and come to the aid of French's division that was unsuccessfully trying to protect the flank of a shattered and retreating force commanded by General John Sedgewick. As Richardson's division went toward the sound of battle the Irish Brigade was in the lead, with the 29th Massachusetts, 63rd New York, 69th New York and 88th New York in column of fours. General Meagher, already noted as "a primper," was wearing a fancy blue uniform with gold shoulder sash, according to Colonel James J. Smith, 69th New York.

Above: *Federal supply depot on the Plains of Manassas, near an abandoned artillery position. A Federal officer is seated on a cracker box next to an old fire site. Behind him is an embrasure for an artillery piece, flanked by gabions filled with dirt. Damaged wagons line the railroad embankment on the right and a train is motionless on the tracks. In the far distance is another fortification and in between are storage sheds and wagon parks, each housing equipment and material necessary to keep the army supplied in the field.*

The brigade ran at the double quick and soon encountered shattered elements of French's division going to the rear on the Roulette Farm. At that point, about 10:00 AM, the order was given to go into assault formation, with the 69th New York on the right and 88th New York on the left. The regiments were by then under small arms fire and General Meagher ordered the men to lie down while volunteers went forward and tore down a sturdy split rail fence some 300 yards to their front in the line of the advance.

Meagher, his staff and two chaplains, Fathers Corby and Ovellet, meanwhile rode calmly along the front rank of the regiments in line, seemingly oblivious to the increasing small arms fire. Father Corby offered conditional absolution to those who would die in the coming assault, except for those who showed cowardice. Meagher then shouted orders to the brigade, "Boys! Raise the colors and follow me!"[16]

Brevet Major General St. Clair Mulholland described the charge of the Irish Brigade across the Roulette Farm cornfield: "As they went on the double quick over the cornstalks, crash came a volley on the right of the line, and the Twenty-ninth (Massachusetts) got a dose. The Sixty-third caught it; the Eighty-eighth coming up in time to get its share of the first course of the heavy repast that was to ensue. This was followed by a brief rest in the deep furrows of the field with sharpshooters busy picking off great numbers of our men."

Above: *Brigadier General Meagher leads the 69th New York Volunteer Infantry against Confederate positions in a sunken road bordering the Roulette Farm. The Second (Tiffany) Irish colors and National colors float above the heads of the men as they advance, and Father Corby grants them conditional absolution should they die bravely in combat. General Meagher's horse will be killed beneath him, and the general will be carried unconscious from the field.*

The rebels were entrenched and screened in a sunken road, all the time pouring a deadly fire into the advancing column of the brigade. The green flag was completely riddled and lay trailing in the dust. It appeared certain death to any one to bear it, for eight color-bearers had already fallen. When Meagher called out his battle cry, Captain James McGee, of the 69th, rushed forward, and crying, "I'll follow you!", seized the flag. As he raised it, a bullet cut the staff in two in his hand; and as he again stooped to pick it up, another bullet tore through his cap. Still, he jumped up, waved the flag, shook it at the rebels, and cheered on the troops.[17]

The actual assault by the brigade struck at that portion of the sunken road that ran along the southern edge of the Roulette Farm defended by G. B. Anderson's North Carolina Brigade, the 2nd, 14th, 4th and 30th North Carolina Regiments, and elements of Carnot Posey's brigade, including the 16th Mississippi on the right flank. The banks that formed the sides of the sunken road made a perfect breastworks for the Confederate infantrymen.[18]

The Confederates were well protected in the road while the assaulting Union troops were crossing an open field. The Union troops closed to within fifty yards of the Confederate position, a range at which their .69 caliber smoothbore muskets loaded with buck and ball were deadly, and fired volley after volley, standing and loading and firing, all the while totally exposed to the accurate fire coming from the entrenched southerners. General Meagher, still mounted, close to the 69th, ordered his men to keep up their fire and then charge the Confederate position. Meagher's uniform was reportedly shot full of holes. His horse was killed under him and the general was thrown violently to the ground. Meagher was knocked senseless by the fall and was carried to the rear.[19] Colonel John Burke, commanding the 63rd New York, assumed command of the brigade at this time.

The heavily engaged Irish regiments soon ran out of ammunition and ceased fire. On command, those men still able rose to their feet, formed in columns of four by regiment, at the right shoulder shift, and prepared to leave the battlefield, still under heavy fire. After some initial confusion and even more casualties, they marched to the rear to a reserve position about 500 yards away, in good order but leaving a big gap in the Federal line.[20] The 61st and 64th New York, Caldwell's Brigade, under Colonel Francis Barlow, resumed the assault, supported by the 7th New York, 81st Pennsylvania and 5th New Hampshire, and forced the surviving North Carolinians out of the sunken road around 1:00 in the afternoon.[21]

General Meagher recovered consciousness about an hour later but was obviously badly shaken. The brigade, after refilling cartridge boxes, returned to their position in front of the sunken road about 1:00 PM, after the action had moved elsewhere, and were not further engaged.[22] Later that day General Richardson was badly wounded by a shell fragment, and Major General Winfield Scott Hancock succeeded him in command of the division.

Meagher and the Irish Brigade were commended by General Sumner in official dispatches. "The brigade sustained its reputation for utter bravery in the face of heavy small arms and artillery fire."[23] The four regiments of the brigade suffered 540 casualties, about 200 each in the 63rd and 69th New York, approximately 60percent, during less than three hours of action.[24]

Both armies remained on the field in defensive posture on September 18. During the night of September 19 and early morning of the following day Lee and the Confederate army fell back across the

> "The Rebels must have been very short of missiles, when they fire off old sledges, horse-shoes, old iron; and in one instance a mule of ours was struck with the leg of a cooking stove! They must have also been short of shells – otherwise, they would not have fired so many solid shot."
>
> From a letter by an unknown officer of the 63rd New York after the Battle of Antietam, September 1862 (Source: *The Irish Brigade*, by Steven J. Wright)

Below: *The sunken road has now earned its new name "Bloody Lane." Ordnance teams have already gathered all weapons.*

Potomac to Virginia and safety, leaving McClellan empty handed. The Irish Brigade marched to Harpers Ferry and camped on Bolivar Heights.

President Lincoln, accompanied by several state governors and members of his staff, visited General McClellan on October 1. The president reviewed the troops on horseback in the company of Generals McClellan, Howard, Hancock and Meagher, and visited the field at Antietam.[25] During this visit plans for further operations against Lee's army must have been the primary topic between McClellan and the increasingly frustrated president.

While at Harpers Ferry on October 9, the Irish Brigade was assigned another regiment, a most welcome addition, the 116th Pennsylvania Volunteers. It was an Irish regiment from the Philadelphia area, under the command of Colonel Dennis Heenan. Shortly thereafter, the brigade, refreshed and refitted, marched to Charlestown and then back to Bolivar Heights, which proved relatively uneventful.

Toward the end of October the Union army moved to the vicinity of Warrenton, Virginia, presumably in preparation to go into winter quarters. The men were aware of rumors of another change in command, and on November 7, 1862, President Lincoln relieved General McClellan and appointed Major General Ambrose P. Burnside in his stead. This change created considerable consternation throughout the army and was the cause of many resignations. A number of officers of the Irish Brigade threatened to resign and some did. General Meagher promptly declined to accept these resignations and subsequently issued an order denouncing such action.[26]

Other changes were occurring that were more pertinent to the brigade. The army was moving base to Falmouth, across the Rappahannock River from Fredericksburg, the land gateway to Richmond. By mid-November replacements were joining the depleted Irish regiments. The move was accomplished in the midst of winter rains that turned the Virginia roads to a clinging, viscous material that slowed the army to a crawl. The division commander, General Hancock, had issued strict orders to respect all private property along the route of march. This meant that the regiments could not tear down roadside fences for firewood. It was a long, cold, uncomfortable march that the men would not forget.

As the brigade was nearing the end of the movement, near Hartwood Church, a Confederate battery was discovered on the

Below right: *The same area of "Bloody Lane," with some of the Confederate dead already removed. Again, no weapons are visible but several cartridge boxes are among the remaining debris of war seen in the roadbed.*

Bottom: *Confederate dead at Antietam, probably of Starke's Louisiana Brigade, along the west side of the Hagerstown Pike near the Miller Farm. These casualties occurred to the north of the area traversed by the Irish Brigade.*

other side of the river. General Sumner happened to be nearby and ordered elements of the Irish Brigade to charge the position. Without hesitation the men quickly ran through the shallow water and captured two guns, the crews being so surprised that they abandoned their weapons and retreated without firing a shot. Major General Hancock, commanding II Corps, also observed the action and, approaching the commanding officer of the Irish Brigade, said, "General Meagher, I have never seen anything so splendid."[27] Generals Sumner, Hancock and Meagher all observed that the river at that time and point posed no barrier and could easily be crossed. The brigade shortly thereafter arrived at Falmouth and began establishing a semi-permanent winter camp.

"The Bloody Lane was the witness of the efficacy of the buck-and-ball at close quarters. We carried the way and the way beyond, leaving on the ground a lot of flags which we were too busy to pick up, for the capture of which Medals of Honor were freely bestowed on the men of another regiment, whose commander was an able performer on the trumpet of self-laudation."

Colonel James J. Smith in a history of the 69th New York.
(Source: *The Irish Brigade*, by Steven J. Wright)

Upon his arrival before Fredericksburg on November 17, Major General Sumner demanded the surrender of the town, but received no response. The new commanding general, Burnside, ordered the city to surrender on November 21, and then did nothing. Sumner ordered occupation of the town but Burnside countermanded his order and told him to wait until the pontoon bridges came up.[28] As the Irish Brigade had already proved, the river could easily be forded at any number of places with little resistance.

Another great opportunity was lost, considered by some to be the saddest blunder of Burnside's military career. The Federal Army sat in the mud and rain on Stafford Heights on the north side of the river and watched General Lee build fortifications for nearly three weeks, the Union forces making no effort to disrupt the work. The common soldiers well understood the nature of Confederate fortifications, and the impossible assault that would be expected of them. While the Irish Brigade watched the Confederate fortifications get stronger by the day the 29th Massachusetts, which had previously served with the brigade, was transferred to duty with IX Corps. In return, the 28th Massachusetts officially became part of the Irish Brigade on November 23, to the satisfaction of all concerned.[29]

Above: *President Abraham Lincoln meets with General McClellan at the headquarters of General Fitz-John Porter, commanding V Corps, about a mile west of Sharpsburg, October 3, 1862, two weeks after the battle. The president spent several days there and conferred with McClellan at some length. There was no question that the commander-in-chief was again unhappy with McClellan's absolute lack of any aggressive pursuit of General Lee's army. This was McClellan's second chance and his performance was unsatisfactory. A month later he was directed to return home to Trenton, New Jersey, "to await orders" that never came. The president's height is quite obvious in this image, as is the short stature of General McClellan.*

While observing the Confederates busily fortifying their positions day after day one Irish soldier is reported to have said to a priest, "Father, are they going to lead us in front of those guns which we have seen them placing unhindered, for the past three weeks?" The priest replied, "Do not trouble yourself; your generals know better than that."[30] General Burnside's pontoon bridges arrived on November 27, before Confederate forces even occupied the town, but the construction of the bridges was delayed until the early hours of the morning of December 11, two weeks later. By then, elements of Confederate Brigadier General William Barksdale's Mississippi Brigade had fortified houses and dug concealed rifle pits covering the riverbank..

The 17th and 50th New York Engineers were assigned the task of throwing the bridges across the river. The Mississippi marksmen, concealed in their prepared positions, shot them to pieces every time men appeared on the riverbank. In an effort to dislodge Barksdale's men

Irish Brigade

> "We have fought the enemy, and our brigade has been cut to pieces! Every man in my company has either been killed or wounded, with the exception of eleven. I received a rifle shot through the left thigh, going completely through – fortunately without touching the bone. Poor Lieut. Henry McConnell was shot through the brain, and never spoke again. P. W. Lyndon, my First Lieutenant, was shot through the heart.... All the line officers of our regiment are either killed or wounded, save one Captain and five Lieutenants."
>
> From a letter by Captain Michael O'Sullivan, Co. F, 63rd New York.
> (Source: *The Irish Brigade*, by Steven J. Wright)

Above: *The monument to the Irish Brigade at Antietam battlefield, Sharpsburg, Maryland. It depicts the assault of the brigade, led by the Irish colors, against Confederate positions.*

Right: *19th century sketch titled "The Fight in the Cornfield. The Irish Brigade Driving the Rebels Out on the Right Wing," showing elements of the Irish Brigade charging across the Roulette Farm fields, assaulting Confederate positions in the sunken road adjacent to the Piper cornfield, defended by the North Carolina Brigade, about mid-morning, September 17, 1862.*

Below: *Proudly depicting the shamrock, the monument of the 132nd Pennsylvania Volunteer Infantry at Antietam.*

and elements of Florida units assisting them, Union artillery began to shell the buildings close to the river, with no appreciable effect.

By noon, Burnside saw his plans becoming as ineffectual as his predecessor's, and ordered a general bombardment of the town with every available gun on Stafford Heights, a total of 147 pieces of artillery of various calibers. After a two-hour bombardment the town was a shambles, with buildings on fire, but Barksdale's men maintained their positions and were still full of fight. By mid-afternoon it became apparent even to Burnside that an amphibious assault was the only option, to force a river crossing. He asked for volunteers to undertake the hazardous mission. Two small regiments, about four hundred men of the 7th Michigan and 19th Massachusetts, were selected to make the crossing.[31] After a spirited firefight the Confederates disengaged and pulled back through Fredericksburg's demolished homes to their main line of battle position on the heights beyond the town, allowing the Federal troops to spend the rest of December 11 and the following day marshaling troops in the ruins of the town.

Above: *Major James Cavanaugh, 69th New York Volunteer Infantry. Major Cavanaugh succeeded Colonel Nugent in command of the regiment after Nugent was wounded and carried from the field. Subsequently, Major Cavanaugh was wounded too. The regiment eventually left the bloody field under its fourth commander, sixteen of its nineteen officers having been killed or wounded in the ill-fated assault on the stonewall on Marye's Heights.*

Below: *Ruins of the houses of Fredericksburg after the bombardment by Federal cannon sited on Stafford Heights across the Rappahannock River on December 11, 1862.*

General Meagher, with the 69th New York in the lead, took the brigade toward the river. After numerous stops and starts, typical of any army, the brigade halted in the open in the drizzling rain and camped for the night. Soldiers slept on rubber ground cloths under wet blankets in the ever-present mud. They were up at 5:00 AM on December 12, and at about 10:30 AM, with the 116th Pennsylvania in the van, were ordered at the double quick down the bank, across the upper bridge into the town, where the brigade deployed on Water Street adjacent to the riverfront. The men of the brigade, knowing full well what they would do the following day, spent the remainder of this day exploring the ruins of the town, cooking rations, and watching the other regiments cross the river under the now active and accurate fire of Confederate artillery.

Most of the brigade got little sleep because of excitement and the periodic explosions caused by artillery. Most were up at 4:00 AM and all were cooking by 6:00. Soon, incessant volleys of musketry were heard that indicated the assault by French's division of about 6,000 men on the Confederate lines on Marye's Heights. The firing reached a crescendo and then almost ceased.

The brigade was sheltered in town and the men could not see the battlefield, but they learned quickly that French's division had been essentially destroyed. By 9:00 AM casualties from French's shattered units began passing the brigade position on their way to medical facilities. What had started as a clear, sunny day suddenly became dark and cloudy. General Hancock appeared in the street and ordered the brigade to "Fall in." General Meagher followed him immediately and issued the same order, and the men checked loaded muskets and aligned formation.

At this point occurred one of the most memorable incidents of the war. General Meagher returned to the street followed by several orderlies

Above: *Colonel Robert Nugent, 69th New York, in a field uniform rather than "dressed to the nines" for photograph. He wears an officer's hat cord around his neck in lieu of a cravat, and a bold checkered shirt.*

Below right: *Private William McCarter's incredible souvenir of the Battle of Fredericksburg: preserved in a labeled bottle, the sprig of boxwood he wore on his hat the day he sustained multiple wounds charging Marye's Heights with the 116th Pennsylvania. This and his diary, of major significance to the story of the Irish Brigade, were discovered in the 1990s.*

carrying large bunches of cut green boxwood. The general remained mounted and did not come closer to the men but sent the orderlies to all the officers with the boxwood sprigs, asking them to present them from him to each man in the ranks. He asked that each man place the sprig of green on his hat before the assault so that he would go into battle with a symbol of Irish green.[32] Small wreaths were made of boxwood and hung on the tattered national flags of the three New York regiments, their bullet-riddled Irish green flags having been sent home for safe keeping.

As the brigade moved through town it was subjected to intermittent artillery fire that inflicted casualties. General Meagher appeared, galloping down one side of the brigade and then up the other side as it marched. The brigade moved up Water Street and turned left on George Street toward the objective, Marye's Heights. General Meagher led the brigade to the field but did not accompany the attack. He had developed a lame leg caused by "an ulcer of the knee joint" and remained at the base of the hill near the canal. Colonel Robert Nugent was the senior officer in the assault.

The brigade crossed a canal some fifteen feet wide on several narrow bridges, although some men waded across, and then reformed regiments in line. The 116th Pennsylvania formed the left flank of the brigade, with the 63rd New York, 28th Massachusetts which had the only green flag as center guide in the middle, and the 88th New York and 69th New York on the far right. Then the order to "Fix Bayonets" was heard up and down the line, followed by "Irish Brigade, Advance, Forward, Double-quick, Guide Center."

Confederate skirmishers fell back from two fencerows to the main line of resistance as the brigade advanced steadily over the field littered with dead and wounded from previous assaults. A London *Times* correspondent wrote to his paper, "Never at Fontenoy, Albuera, or at Waterloo was more undoubted courage displayed by the sons of Erin

"You doubtless remember when we assaulted 'Marye's' Heights, ('Fredericksburg') Dec. 13, 1862[,] the soldiers of the Irish Brigade placed little sprigs of 'green' in their caps just before the order was given to advance to the attack. The Brigade had stacked arms in the street. A house near by was overgrown with an evergreen vine, box I believe, and each man of the Irish Brigade passed over it and pulling off a bit of the green stuck it in the front of his cap. In a few moments afterwards the word was given for the assault and very soon a number of the gallant fellows lay dead and wounded with the little green sprigs on their heads."

From a letter to Second Army Corps historian Francis A. Walker from W. G. Mitchell, of Maj. Gen. Winfield Scott Hancock's staff, in 1883. (Source: *The Irish Brigade*, by Steven J. Wright)

"Right gallantly the Irishmen charge over the sheltering ridge, and dash across the bloody spaces strewn with the dead and dying of the brigades that have gone on before....The killed and wounded fall like leaves in the autumn, while hundreds of men, brave among the bravest, lie down beneath the storm of lead. [Colonel Robert] Nugent and [Colonel Patrick] Kelly, to whom the Irish Brigade has become accustomed to look for examples of courage and devotion, are at the front; with their own hands they undertake to tear down fences and make a way to the stone wall."

Francis A. Walker, *History of the Second Army Corps in the Army of the Potomac.*

than during those six frantic dashes which they directed against the almost impregnable position of their foe."[33]

Survivors of the charge estimated that the action lasted no more than half-an-hour. Soldiers who were not killed or wounded lay among the casualties, protected by their bodies, loading muskets on their backs and rolling on their bellies to fire. Cartridges were taken from the boxes of the dead who lay near men who continued to fire until they ran out of ammunition.

The Confederate line initially manned by Cobb's Georgia troops had been reinforced by regiments from the brigades of Brigadier Generals Joseph Kershaw, John R. Cooke, and Robert Ransom. Confederate infantrymen stood four deep in the shelter of the sunken lane and were able to maintain virtually uninterrupted fire on the assaulting Federal troops. The musketry fire began at 9:30 AM and continued without cessation until 6:45 PM. Artillery was placed in the line and above infantry positions on the heights, and had unrestricted fields of fire. Lieutenant Colonel E. Porter Alexander, commanding Confederate artillery during the battle said, "A chicken could not live on that field when we open on it."

The Irish Brigade mustered about 1,700 men going into the assault.[34] Casualties crawled to the rear all day and all night. Early on, General Meagher, still mounted, met fragments of the 63rd and 69th regiments as the men fell back to town. He accompanied survivors of the two regiments across the Rappahannock until he learned that General Hancock had not authorized this movement, and then he quickly brought them back to Fredericksburg.[35] The five regiments had only 263 men fit for duty the following day.[36]

Left: *The Irish and National colors of the 28th Massachusetts lead the Irish Brigade in their intrepid but doomed assault against the impregnable Confederate lines on Marye's Heights at Fredericksburg.*

Above: *The Grand Requiem Mass held in St. Patrick's Cathedral in New York City on January 16, 1863, for the deceased officers and men of the Irish Brigade.*

Opposite page: *Men of the 116th Pennsylvania Regiment, actually a very under-strength battalion commanded by reduced-in-rank Major Mulholland, drag the Parrott rifles of the 5th Maine Battery off the field under heavy fire near the Chancellor House, to prevent capture by victorious Confederate troops.*

Below: *The reviewing stand at the steeple-chase hosted by the Irish Brigade on St. Patrick's Day, 1863. Major General Joe Hooker and 30,000 officers and men attended this social event of the season.*

Even after the decimation of the Irish Brigade, General Burnside ordered additional attacks over the same ground for the remainder of the day. No fewer than fourteen full-scale assaults were made on the stone wall. By nightfall the ground in front of the wall was covered with dead and wounded Union troops. Those closest to the wall had green sprigs of boxwood on their caps.

The Battle of Fredericksburg left General Meagher virtually without a command. The survivors failed to muster an under-strength regiment. Yet, the day after the slaughter, Meagher and other members of the brigade commandeered a theater in Fredericksburg and invited guests from throughout the army to attend an enormous banquet and celebrate the presentation of new green flags to regiments that hardly now existed, all the while under fire from Confederate guns only a mile away.[37]

The shattered brigade went into winter camp at Falmouth on December 16, 1862, and remained there until April 27, 1863. During that time General Joseph Hooker assumed command of the demoralized Army of the Potomac on January 25, 1863, and Burnside was sent west to the Department of the Ohio, out of harm's way.

Concurrently, General Meagher was pursuing his own agenda. On January 1 he requested a twenty-day leave for medical reasons, but when his leave expired on January 21 he failed to report for duty. On February 3 he wrote directly to the Adjutant General of the Army advising that his health had not improved but he would report at Washington on February 11. On that day, ignoring the chain of command, General Meagher personally visited President Lincoln and requested that the Irish Brigade be relieved to return home so as to recruit and refit.[38] Then, on February 19, Meagher, again disregarding the chain of command, wrote directly to the Secretary of War, making an official request for inactive duty on behalf of what was left of the Irish Brigade. General Hooker flatly refused to endorse the request.

While still in winter quarters, on March 16, 1863, the remnants of the Irish Brigade hosted St. Patrick's Day festivities that were never forgotten in the Army of the Potomac. Even though there was friction between Hooker and Meagher, the commanding general attended the holiday billed as the Grand Irish Brigade Steeple-Chase. David Power Conyngham described the preparations thus: "The Quartermaster was sent to Washington for liquors and meats, and brought for the banquet that was to follow the race the following moderate supply, which constituted the fare; thirty-five hams, and a side of ox roasted; an entire pig, stuffed with boiled turkeys; an unlimited number of chickens, ducks and small game. The drinking materials comprised eight baskets of champagne, ten gallons of rum and twenty-two gallons of whiskey mixed in to some form of punch the night before the festivities and served from an enormous bowl holding not much less than thirty gallons."[39] Activities included a steeple-chase, foot races, sack races, wheelbarrow races and a greased-pig chase. To start the festivities, each man in the brigade received two gills of whiskey.

> "Soon nothing was left near the Chancellorsville house except the Irish Brigade and the almost silenced battery. One gun was still firing, however, and a gallant corporal and one man still clung to the piece and fired it when all others had gone. It was time for the last troops to fall back, and the order came to the 116th Pennsylvania volunteers to save the abandons [sic] guns. One hundred of the men were soon detailed to rush forward and surround the pieces and drag them to the rear, which was done in splendid style."

St. Clair A. Mulholland in a postwar newspaper article, describing the Battle of Chancellorsville and the salvaging of the 5th Maine battery's guns. (Source: *The Irish Brigade*, by Steven J. Wright)

After the festivities General Meagher requested additional leave. He advised his commanding officer, General Hancock, that an attack of rheumatism prevented him from attending to his duties and that he must go to Baltimore or Philadelphia for treatment. His good friend, Surgeon Frank Reynolds, obligingly wrote the required medical certificate.

The brigade remained in camp at Falmouth until Meagher's return and then participated in the Chancellorsville Campaign. At the outset of the campaign the brigade only had 520 men, sadly under-strength, with morale at an all time low. The campaign commenced on April 27, when the brigade broke camp and led II Corps toward United States Ford. General Meagher was with the 116th Pennsylvania, 69th New York and 28th Massachusetts during this march. A pontoon bridge was put across the ford and II Corps crossed unopposed.

Subsequently, the brigade was ordered to protect Bank's Ford until May 2, when the brigade was ordered to support the 5th Maine Artillery close by the Chancellor House. After the gun crews were killed or wounded, or abandoned the guns, elements of the brigade, 116th Pennsylvania under the command of Major Mulholland, hauled the guns by hand for three miles to prevent capture by Confederate forces. Meagher's brigade also acted to prevent panic-stricken retreating soldiers from routing the whole army.

Later, General Hancock ordered Meagher and the Irish Brigade to protect the retreat of the army from Chancellorsville.[41] Mulholland was awarded the Medal of Honor for his actions on May 5. The brigade had about 500 men when it went to support the Maine artillery and lost over 100 to artillery fire during their engagement

Repeated requests to the War Department for relief for recruitment and refitting had been denied. Now, after the Battle of Chancellorsville, Meagher had lost 20percent of his remaining force. The general again asked to have his brigade relieved since it had been reduced to a battalion of a few hundred men, but he was again denied.

Brigadier General Thomas Francis Meagher tendered his resignation on May 8, 1863, to Secretary of War Edwin Stanton. It was accepted on May 14, 1863. Meagher said goodbye to the remaining 400 men of the brigade on May 19 and turned over command to Colonel Patrick Kelly, 88th New York. Then Meagher returned to his home in New York.[42]

Chapter 5

Demise and Rebirth

General Meagher's farewell to the remnants of the Irish Brigade was a very emotional and memorable event. The brigade was drawn up in a square surrounding the general. The eloquent Irishman reminisced about the fabled exploits of the brigade and then shook the hand of each officer. Meagher then trooped the line and shook the hand of every enlisted man in the ranks. The farewell of the general – strangely reminiscent of Napoleon's farewell to his marshals and the Old Guard at Fontainebleau in 1814 – together with the staggering losses of the last few months did nothing to help the sagging morale of the brigade.[1] Colonel Patrick Kelly, the new brigade commander, dismissed the formation to resume the mundane camp duties in the bivouac near Falmouth.

In early June 1863 General Lee's Army of Northern Virginia began moving north toward Maryland and Pennsylvania. General Hooker and the

"The brigade were kneeling and our faithful Chaplain, Father Corby, invoked the Divine blessing on their cause and undertaking. Rising from that posture, the command 'Forward!' is heard along the line; and fortified with religious consolation the Irish Brigade advanced, carrying the Stars and Stripes and the old Green Flag of Erin – the two flags they had already followed through so many battlefields. On and through the wheat that covered the ground, they advanced gradually and surely, losing many of their number, until out of the 530 who advanced, 195 are killed and wounded before they are brought to a halt."

Denis F. Bourke, at the dedication of Irish Brigade monuments at Gettysburg, after the war.
(Source: *The Irish Brigade*, by Steven J. Wright)

Below: *Wood's painting, Absolution Under Fire, shows Father Corby standing on a rock giving absolution to the remnants of the Irish Brigade, with General Hancock and staff, mounted, in the distance. Moments later the brigade dashed into the Wheatfield, and disaster.*

Army of the Potomac began the race north to keep between Confederate forces and Washington. With Lee having been so successful so far, it seemed inevitable that when these great armies would collide again it would be on Northern territory, and it would be soon. The epic battle that was looming was to bestow everlasting fame on a previously little known crossroads in Pennsylvania – Gettysburg.

Opposite page: *After the battles the remains of the hastily or partly buried casualties were gathered for possible identification and more permanent internment. Here, months after the suicidal assault at Cold Harbor, crews gather the decomposed skeletons. Colonel Richard Byrnes, 28th Massachusetts, commanding, was mortally wounded here and the brigade suffered heavy casualties.*

Above: *Major General George Gordon Meade assumed command of the army just days before the Battle of Gettysburg where the brigade was badly mauled.*

Above: *Colonel Patrick Kelly, 88th New York Volunteers, assumed command of the Irish Brigade after Chancellorsville and Meagher's resignation. He led the small brigade into the Wheatfield at Gettysburg.*

On June 14 II Corps and the Irish Brigade began the long march. At this time the three New York regiments had been consolidated into three battalions with only two companies in each battalion, a total strength of 240 officers and men. The 116th Pennsylvania mustered one company of 66 effectives. The 28th Massachusetts had the most men with 224. For over two weeks the battered brigade of only 530 men force-marched with a few days of scattered rest, trying to keep up with Lee's army. During this intense race the route of march went through the old battlefields around Bull Run. The already demoralized soldiers were greeted by the grinning skulls of partially buried remains of soldiers and the scattered debris of war that did nothing to improve their disposition.

While in Frederick, Maryland, on June 28, the brigade heard the news of yet another change of command of the Army of the Potomac. Hooker was gone. Now their commanding officer was Major General George Gordon Meade, formerly commander of the V Corps.[2] The exhausted men of the Irish Brigade arrived in the vicinity of Gettysburg the evening of July 1 after the first day of the epic battle's action there had ceased. They went into the left center of the Union line on Cemetery Ridge, with II Corps under Major General Winfield Scott Hancock.

The next morning was uneventful and the division remained massed in columns of brigades.[3] The Irishmen rested in formation and watched with interest the movement of troops in the immediate area. About 1:00 PM Union Major General Daniel Sickles advanced his III Corps forward, toward the Peach Orchard and the Emmitsburg Road, forming a projecting salient in front of the existing Union line. General Hancock happened to be nearby with the senior officers of the Irish Brigade and observed the whole episode in amazement. No one in their group was aware of any movement orders issued by General Meade and the III Corps was assuming a very exposed position.

Suddenly, out of the woods across the road, General James Longstreet's I Corps, almost 15,000 troops, struck the exposed Union troops. The battle was intense and see-sawed back and forth for four hours. Eventually, Sickle's men began falling back in some disorder. Hancock received orders to send a division to protect the exposed flank caused by Sickle's precipitous forward movement, and he directed Brigadier General John C. Caldwell to take his small division composed of the Irish Brigade and three other under-strength brigades to support Sickle's III Corps. It was then about 4:30 PM.

Here occurred another incredible incident in the long chain of memorable events associated with the Irish Brigade. By this time the brigade was under artillery and scattered small arms fire. Father Corby, attached to the 88th New York, the only priest on the battlefield, spontaneously climbed up on a rock, put his purple stole around his neck, and began giving absolution to the Irishmen about to go into battle. The whole brigade became quiet, took off their headgear and knelt down

"We had hardly got under way when the enemy's batteries opened and shells began falling all around us. The ground on which this division faced the enemy the afternoon of the 2d had already been fought over again and again, and the field and woods were strewn with killed or wounded.

As we approached the crest of the rugged hill, from behind the huge boulders that were everywhere scattered around, the men of Longstreet's corps rose up and poured into our ranks a most destructive fire. The sudden meeting astonished us, the lines being not more than thirty feet apart when the firing opened. I cannot imagine why the rebs allowed us to get so near before firing, unless they thought we would give way under the weight and impulse of the attack.

Our men promptly returned the fire, and for ten or fifteen minutes the work of death went on. There was no cheering, no time lost in unnecessary movement. Every man there, both Union and rebel, were veterans, and knew just what was wanted. They stood there face to face, loading and firing, and so close that every shot told.

They fired down while our men fired upward, and our fire was more effective.

On their line we found many dead but few wounded – they were nearly all hit in the head or the upper part of the body. Behind one rock I counted five dead bodies. This was some of the most severe fighting our division had ever done, and was so close that the officers used their revolvers."

St. Clair A. Mulholland on the Irish Brigade's action at Gettysburg, in an article for the *Philadelphia Times* series "Annals of the War." (Source: *The Irish Brigade*, by Steven J. Wright)

WHEATFIELD

Above: *The 19-acre Wheatfield at Gettysburg as it looks nearly a century and a half after the battered remnants of the Irish Brigade crashed into superior numbers of Brigadier General Joseph B. Kershaw's South Carolina troops in a strong position along the edge of the field. Opposing forces were so close to each other that officers used their revolvers. Elements of another Confederate brigade flanked the Irishmen, and Kelly's men were forced to run a gauntlet of deadly Confederate fire in their precipitous withdrawal.*

Previous page: *Other Irishmen fought under the green flag beside those of the Irish Brigade. At Gettysburg, the 69th Pennsylvania, part of the Philadelphia Brigade, bore the brunt of Longstreet's Assault (Pickett's Charge) at the Angle near the Copse of Trees on July 3, 1863. Both brigades served in the II Corps and wore the trefoil corps badge on the forage cap. Like the Irish Brigade, the Philadelphia Brigade and the 69th Pennsylvania had been drastically reduced in numbers by mid-1863 but the 69th Pennsylvania still carried their green flag at the Battle of Gettysburg. The Irish Brigade's flags had long since been sent home for safekeeping. The stalwart bravery of the Irishmen of the Philadelphia Brigade at Gettysburg was the same caliber as that of their kinsman in the Irish Brigade at Fredericksburg.*

in the midst of the battle raging around them. Major Mulholland, 116th Pennsylvania, said it was awe-inspiring. General Hancock and his staff, then mounted, uncovered their heads, while the brief service continued.[4] It was over in a short moment, and the brigade moved off to enter the battle, but the incident has become one of the cornerstones of the legend surrounding the Irish Brigade. It is the subject of the famous painting by Paul Henry Wood, *Absolution Under Fire*.

Colonel Kelly led his small brigade at right shoulder shift in line of regiments into a waist-high field of wheat, following Brigadier General Zook's brigade. The Irishman were in the open when General Kershaw's 3rd and 7th South Carolina opened fire on them from their strong defensive positions along the edge of the Wheatfield. However, the outnumbered Irish Brigade actually took the South Carolinian's position and prepared to defend it, but the Irishmen were surprised by a flank assault from another Confederate brigade, together with the reappearance of Kershaw's men on their other flank. Ordered to retire rather than surrender, the already depleted brigade had to run a gauntlet of Confederate fire back through the Wheatfield. Those who survived reformed near the Taneytown Road. The brigade had lost 202 men, almost 40percent of the force it mustered at the beginning of the action. The remaining members of the brigade resumed their defensive position and, while they saw no further action at Gettysburg, they had a spectacular view of the repulse of Confederate General Longstreet's assault on the last day of the battle, July 3.

Under the weight of superior Union firepower and with the excellent Federal defensive positions withstanding the Confederates' grand frontal

Below: *The eastern slope of Little Round Top, near the southern end of the Federal line. This high ground was General Longstreet's objective in his assault on the afternoon of July 2. The Irish Brigade and other battered Federal units retreated in that direction, crossing "an alley of death," as Major Mulholland described it. The Brigade numbered only 530 men going into the Wheatfield, and 195 of them were killed or wounded in the action.*

Bottom: *Present-day view from the forward slope of Little Round toward the Confederate positions. Survivors of the encounter in the Wheatfield fell back toward the security of this high ground to the Federal line along the Taneytown Road. Later that evening the brigade re-occupied its former positions on the left of the II Corps on Cemetery Ridge.*

assault, General Lee's battered Army of Northern Virginia suffered a crushing defeat, and the survivors began the long trek back to Virginia on the night of July 4. General Meade and the Union Army were too exhausted to aggressively follow the retiring Confederates. The bloodiest battle in American history had cost each side more than 20,000 in dead and wounded.

The Irish Brigade was so shattered that it was combat ineffective, a handful of companies, but the men stayed with II Corps through the marches and actions of late summer and early fall. On October 14, Lieutenant Louis J. Sacriste, commanding officer of the rear guard covering the withdrawal of II Corps at Auburn Creek, so distinguished himself in a day-long, running engagement that he was recommended for and received the Medal of Honor. Subsequently, the brigade went into camp around Centreville for a period of light duty and recuperation.

On November 9 Thomas Francis Meagher, out of uniform in civilian dress, visited the Irish Brigade at Shakelsfords Farm. He stayed with the brigade for several days and it was just like old times, "first class jollification."[5] Shortly thereafter, the brigade was reviewed by Marshal Prim of the Spanish Army, followed by a day of camp sports and horse racing, and this was followed by a visit from Colonel Peel of the British Grenadier Guards, who stayed for several days.

At the end of November the brigade was engaged during the short Mine Run campaign, in which General Meade attempted to turn the flank of the Confederate forces. Slow and possibly inept execution of movement orders allowed General Lee ample time to establish strong defensive positions, and Meade wisely withdrew rather than squander his resources. The Irish Brigade was later detailed to guard the ammunition train carrying ordnance for the whole army, a position of relative safety, relieving the unit from actual combat duty. It then went into winter camp at Stevensburg, three miles from Brandy Station. An endless series of pickets, drills and reviews occupied the Irishmen's time. Meanwhile, some of the officers returned home to recruit new men for the skeleton brigade.

Above: *Bronze statue of Father Corby, sculpted by Samuel Aloysius Murray, at the site of the absolution incident. General Mulholland began plans to erect the statue in 1890 but lack of funds prevented progress. Corby died in December 1897 but Mulholland persevered and finally got the Catholic Alumni Sodality of Philadelphia to raise funds in 1909. Mulholland died in February 1910; the project was competed in October of that year.*

Opposite top: *The Irish Brigade Monument erected at Gettysburg to the memory of the 63rd, 69th and 88th New York Regiments. The Celtic cross, on which is emblazoned the trefoil badge of the II Corps, indicates the origin of most of the brigade.*

Opposite bottom: *The Monument of the 28th Massachusetts Volunteers erected in 1885. Of the five regiments of the Irish Brigade only the 28th Massachusetts had sufficient numbers to be called a regiment. The 63rd, 69th and 88th New York and the 116th Pennsylvania had only two companies each and together hardly made a battalion.*

Over the holidays the veterans of the brigade were asked to re-enlist for the duration of the war, and were offered bounties and furloughs home as inducement. Almost all the men re-enlisted and the men of the New York regiments arrived in the city on January 2, 1864, but received little welcome. Upon hearing this, a group of senior and former officers formed a committee, chaired by General Meagher (who the previous month had learned that his resignation had been refused). They met at the Whitney House to formulate an appropriate program in recognition of the re-enlisted men and the honorably discharged veterans of the brigade. The committee decided that a grand banquet would be held in honor of the brigade members.

On January 16 the men assembled at City Hall and were reviewed by the Mayor of New York. Then, led by the Wadsworth Band, they marched up Broadway to Irving Hall, the site of the festivities. Veterans disabled by loss of limb were already in attendance and the whole group entered the hall, where five tables ran the length of the hall and seated two hundred enlisted men. The non-commissioned officers sat at a table that ran across the head of the room, with the band on the stage above them. The hall was grandly decorated with the old battle-torn green banners and the newer ones presented by the merchants of New York, together with painted national shields bearing battle honors from Yorktown through Bristoe Station. The gallery was filled with wives, widows and relatives of men of the brigade. General Meagher and the other officers entered and Meagher spoke at some length. His well-received remarks were followed by a long series of toasts, the last being, "The Irish Brigade; what there is left of it."[6]

Recruitment proceeded in Pennsylvania and Massachusetts for the other two regiments and the new men arrived in camp in late February. The 69th New York was filled to its minimum requirements, and the 116th Pennsylvania mustered enough recruits to become a regiment again, no longer a battalion, and Major Mulholland became colonel.[7] While still in winter camp St. Patrick's Day, March 17, 1864, was observed in standard fashion by the Irish Brigade. The new recruits were welcomed to the ranks and General Caldwell, division commander, addressed the guests, after which there were various races and camp sports.[8] The celebration was more subdued than the previous year, and much of the fun and spirit was no longer with the brigade.

Lieutenant General U. S. Grant was given authority to command all Union Armies on March 10. On that day Grant was already in Virginia with

General Meade, establishing a working arrangement with him and planning a decisive spring campaign that would hasten the end of the war.

On May 3 the brigade and II Corps massed near the ruins of the old Chancellor House, and the army crossed the Rapidan River. Colonel Thomas A. Smyth was now brigade commander as the regiments plunged into the Wilderness along the Brock Road. The undergrowth along the road was so thick that regiments could not keep alignment nor see the unit next to them.

The brigade became heavily engaged on May 6 and behaved with remarkable bravery and coolness despite 80percent of the men being new recruits. During the vicious fighting the brush along the Brock Road line caught fire, which added to the intensity of the battle. Visibility was limited by undergrowth and smoke, and many wounded were burned to death in the roaring inferno that sent flames fifteen feet in the air. The brigade maintained its position the next day amid the smoldering woods and charred corpses of the dead. The following day the Irishmen withdrew towards Todd's Tavern and got their first glimpse of General Grant as he rode past. The Irish Brigade moved to the Po River and

was engaged there before making an all night march in chilling rain, arriving at Spotsylvania at 4:30 AM on May 11.

Not for the first time, General Lee anticipated General Grant's objective, and Confederate forces were well entrenched in a strong position known as the Mule Shoe Salient because of its shape. Units of the Federal II Corps were ordered to make a pre-dawn assault on the fortifications. Men of the Irish Brigade were told to draw cartridges, unload their firearms, and make the attack with only their bayonets so as to insure silence and surprise. The Irish Brigade led by Colonel Smyth was in the second line of the assault force that moved stealthily into position. The attack was a complete surprise, catching many of the Confederate defenders still asleep in their tents behind their lines. But the rebels' reaction was swift, and combat became hand to hand.

The momentum of the assault carried the Union force over and into the Confederate works, past the McCool House, and to the reserve line at the base of the salient. But this was where Confederate troops

Above: *Brigadier General Meagher late in the war, in a civilian style coat with military shoulder straps. He has donned his Baldric box and sword belt and has a large unidentified badge on the left breast.*

Opposite page: *Confederate casualties at Spotsylvania. The pre-dawn assault on the salient caught Confederate troops asleep in their tents. Many were taken prisoner but many died in the fierce fight.*

Above: *Captain Pierce Ryder, 88th New York Volunteer Infantry, killed in action May 5, 1864, during savage fighting in the dense, tangled woods of the Wilderness surrounding the intersection of the Orange Plank Road and the Brock Roads.*

contained them and began to drive them back to the Bloody Angle. There, Confederate and Union soldiers fired at each other from each side of the parapet, a distance of a few feet. Small arms fire was so furious that one tree, twenty-two inches in diameter, was cut in two. Fighting continued until nearly midnight. Eventually, Confederate forces retired to the reserve line. The Union's II Corps captured two Confederate general officers, 30 flags, 18 pieces of artillery and 4,000 prisoners. Men of the Irish Brigade were some of the first over the Confederate works, but casualties were high.[9]

Colonel Smyth was reassigned on May 20 and Colonel Richard Byrnes, who had returned from recruiting for the 28th Massachusetts, assumed command of the brigade. The campaign continued day after day and became a routine of one violent assault after another while the Union Army constantly tried to turn the right flank of the dwindling Confederate forces by moving south. Lee somehow managed to keep one step ahead of Grant through May into June, but Grant's "meat-grinder" tactics were slowly wearing the southern forces down. These hard fought battles were having an even more costly effect on Union forces. The Irish Brigade, even with the infusion of new recruits in early spring, had suffered irreplaceable losses in both officers and men.

The Irish regiments were engaged successively at the North Anna, Pamunkey and Totopotomy Rivers during the latter part of May. On June 1, the brigade and II Corps disengaged and marched all night to Cold Harbor, arriving exhausted at 6:30 AM. The corps was too tired and disorganized to assault the Confederate lines immediately, so the attack was postponed until late afternoon and subsequently postponed again until the following morning. Unfortunately, these delays allowed General Lee sufficient time to concentrate all his forces in a seven-mile-long defensive position that made maximum use of favorable topography and allowed extraordinary interlocking and overlapping fields of fire, even stronger than the defenses had been at Fredericksburg.

At 4:30 AM Grant launched his typical frontal assault with 40,000 men along a six-mile front. The Union forces had not a clue of the strength of the Confederate fortifications and were caught completely by surprise. On the Union left elements of Hancock's II Corps momentarily penetrated the Confederate line. The Irish Brigade was in the second line of the assault but its men soon found themselves in the Confederate works under incredibly intense small arms and artillery fire. Colonel Byrnes was mortally wounded, hit in the back near the spine, while trying to withdraw his men from their untenable position. Colonel Patrick Kelly assumed command. The whole Union line was driven back. The Irishmen withdrew and threw up a defensive line. The slaughter was over in about half-an-hour. Grant had lost 7,000 men.[10]

The Union Army again quietly moved south on June 12, through White Oak Swamp, across the James River, and on toward Petersburg. After a long, hard three-day march the brigade entered the lines then

"The men of the One Hundred and Sixteenth were among the first over the works, and the colors of the Regiment were in advance. Personal encounters between individuals took place on every part of the disputed ground. Lieutenant Fraley, of Company F, ran a Confederate color-bearer through with his sword; a Confederate shot one of the men when almost within touch of his musket, then threw down his piece and called out, 'I surrender,' but Dan Crawford, of Company K, shot him dead; Billy Hager, of the same company, ran into a group of half a dozen and demanded their surrender, saying, 'Throw down your arms, quick now, or I'll stick my bayonet into you, and they obeyed. Henry J. Bell, known as 'Binky Bell,' leaped over the works and yelled 'Look out, throw down your arms, we run this machine now.'"

St. Clair A. Mulholland on the hand-to-hand action in the Confederate entrenchments near Spotsylvania, in *The Story of the One Hundred and Sixteenth Regiment Pennsylvania Volunteers in the War of the Rebellion: the Record of a Gallant Command.*

Above (left to right): *Brigadier General Frances C. Barlow commanded the 1st Division, II Corps in which the Irish Brigade served at the battles of the Wilderness and Spotsylvania; Major General David Bell Birney commanded a division that often fought alongside the brigade; Colonel Richard Byrnes, 28th Massachusetts, was mortally wounded leading the brigade during the ill-conceived assault at Cold Harbor in 1864.*

Above: *Captain Garrett Nowlen, Company D and adjutant, posthumously promoted to major, served with distinction but died at Reams' Station, Virginia, August 1864.*

forming around Petersburg, drew rations, and rested. The divisions of Generals Barlow and Birney were in action during the evening of June 16 and the brigade participated in the successful assault on Confederate redans 3, 13 and 14. But the brigade suffered heavy losses, including Colonel Kelly who was killed during the fight. Small unit actions and skirmishing continued daily, and eventually the dwindling brigade was withdrawn and placed in reserve.

The Irish Brigade had started the campaign in May with ten field grade officers. Now, six were dead and the remaining four were wounded in hospital. Enlisted casualties were similarly disheartening. By mid-July the brigade had lost over 1,000 men, was reduced to regimental strength, and was commanded by a captain.

Officer resignations increased and the brigade showed obvious signs of battle fatigue and low morale. Other units had also been decimated by the hard fought spring battles. Therefore, on June 27, 1864, the 2nd Brigade was consolidated with the 3rd Brigade and designated the Consolidated Brigade, 1st Division. The 116th Pennsylvania was reassigned to the Fourth Brigade.[11] The Irish Brigade had ceased to exist.

The Irishmen now assigned to the Consolidated Brigade, commanded by Colonel James E. McGee, remained in the siege lines before Petersburg. Throughout July and August continuous skirmishing occurred, but the dash and élan associated with the original unit was gone. The fight at Ream's Station on August 25 involved elements of the Consolidated Brigade under General Miles. Some of these units retreated and General Gibbon's Division, also involved, behaved poorly. A large number of Union troops were captured.

In early September General Meagher visited the brigade again while on his way to report for duty in rear echelon commands under General

> **"Never has a regimental color of the Irish Brigade graced the halls of its enemies. Let the spirit that animates the officers and men of the present be that which shall strive to emulate the deeds of the old brigade."**
>
> Colonel Robert Nugent of the 69th New York, on assuming command of the Irish Brigade in 1864.

Below: *Colonel Robert Nugent, 69th New York Volunteers. He has a hat insignia with numerals 69 surrounded by a wreath of shamrocks.*

Sherman. A celebration of the founding of the original brigade was held on September 4, with honored guests including Generals Hancock, Birney, Gibbon, Mott, Miles and De Trobriand. Unsurprisingly, General Meagher was in charge of the festivities. Speeches were the order of the day from most of the generals, and there was much gaiety, but once again the old spirit was missing.[12]

The Irish Brigade was reorganized on November 2, 1864, under the command of Colonel Robert Nugent, one of the few surviving original officers. Intensive recruiting had brought the old regiments up to strength. The three New York regiments, the 28th Massachusetts and the 7th New York Heavy Artillery, fighting as infantry, were assigned to make up the new brigade. The 4th New York Heavy Artillery, also fighting as infantry, replaced the latter regiment in March 1865. Hancock was gone from II Corps in November, too, replaced by General A. A. Humphreys who commanded the corps until the end of the war.

The reconstituted brigade with the greatly weakened II Corps soldiered on through the winter in the siege lines around Petersburg. In late March the Appomattox Campaign began, and the new brigade participated in the pursuit of General Lee's army after Petersburg was evacuated on April 2, 1865. It was obvious the war was nearly over when news arrived of the mortal wounding of General Thomas A. Smyth, one of the brigade's old commanders. He was the last general officer killed in the war.[13]

At 8:30 PM on April 7 Colonel Robert Nugent carried General Grant's first letter to General Robert E. Lee suggesting surrender.[14] The brigade with the II Corps was on the march toward Appomattox when news of the surrender of the Army of Northern Virginia reached them. The brigade and the division, then commanded by General Miles, went into camp at Burkesville from April 13 until April 30. Along with the other elements of Grant's army, the brigade moved to Washington, DC, during the period May 2-12, 1865, in preparation for the Grand Review that was held May 23, 1865. The Irish Brigade proudly carried the Second (Tiffany) Colors in that parade.[15] Very few of the soldiers who marched in the final parade had been with the brigade when the colors were presented 1862.

After the last review the brigade disbanded. The New York regiments went home and were mustered out on June 30, 1865. The Irish veterans turned in their tattered flags to

"The famous and now long-tried Irish Brigade, under the command of Brevet Brigadier General Robert Nugent, arrived early yesterday morning, remaining all of yesterday and last night at the Battery, preparatory to taking part in the grand celebration of today. This brigade consists of four regiments, viz: the Sixty-third, Sixty-ninth, and Eighty-eighth New York, and the Twenty-eighth Massachusetts Regiment, from Boston. The brigade has an extensive and gallant record, having shared in the glory of every engagement fought by the army of the Potomac, since its organization, from the siege of Yorktown and the Peninsula campaign, under McClellan, through all the different campaigns of Hooker, Burnside, Meade and Grant, down to the final surrender of the army of northern Virginia, under Lee, at Appomattox Hollow, Va., April 9, 1865."

The New York Times, July 4, 1865. (Source: *The Irish Brigade*, by Steven J. Wright)

respective armories or state repositories, and went home to rebuild their lives. No doubt they carried with them the epitaph that best described the Irish Brigade during the war – the comment that some Irishman made at Gettysburg upon hearing that the brigade was placed in reserve: "In reserve, yes, reserved for the heavy fighting."[16]

Irish veterans became active in veterans' associations and the Grand Army of the Republic from the outset. In 1888 Father Corby attended the 25th Anniversary of the battle of Gettysburg, and thereafter he and General Mulholland became the driving force in memorializing the exploits of the Irish Brigade.

Paul Henry Wood's painting, *Absolution Under Fire*, depicting the brigade at that incredible moment at Gettysburg, was finished on November 14, 1891, and placed at the University of Notre Dame where it resides today. Shortly thereafter Father Corby secured the green flag of the 63rd New York for his projected museum at Notre Dame

Above: *Brigadier General Andrew Atkinson Humphreys, who succeeded Major General Winfield Scott Hancock as commanding officer of II Corps in November 1864 and basically commanded the Corps until the war's end.*

Right: *Captain William H. Terwilliger, seated center with mourning badge on sleeve, commanding the 63rd New York Volunteers, and officers of Company A, in camp near Washington.*

Above: *Officers of the 28th Massachusetts Volunteers in camp after the close of the war. Some wear mourning badges on the left sleeve, for assassinated President Abraham Lincoln. Shortly hereafter the brigade would be disbanded and sent home.*

Right: *Major General Winfield Scott Hancock, commander of II Corps, in which the Irish Brigade fought for most of its illustrious career. Hancock commanded a division at Fredericksburg, including the Irish Brigade, was next to the brigade at Gettysburg during the absolution incident and was Corps commander until late November 1864. He was aware of the fighting qualities of the Irish Brigade and always depended on them.*

commemorating the brigade, but he died in 1897. The statue of Father Corby at Gettysburg was unveiled in 1910 shortly after the death of General Mulholland, who supervised the project, but the die was cast. The brigade would not be forgotten. It has been commemorated by monuments on various battlefields, in literature published since the war and continuing to the present, in a plethora of period paintings, and by living history and reenactment groups dedicated to preserving the memory of the brigade not only in the United States but also overseas. Some of these reenacting groups provide highly visible representations of the Irish Brigade at events held throughout the year. Their exacting standards and attention to historical detail provide an accurate picture of the brigade as it was in the 19th century.

The surviving green flags and national colors, the little sprig of boxwood preserved in a glass bottle, and the painting, *Absolution Under Fire,* together with the swords of Generals Corcoran and Meagher and other three dimensional artifacts scattered in private and public collections around the country have become venerated icons of this historic unit and insure the legacy of the Irish Brigade will ever be remembered.

"Comrades we have seen these two banners wave at Gaines' Mill when despair and defeat were imminent; they waved at Malvern Hill when the ground shook beneath the charging legions of Lee; we have seen them at Antietam breast the shock of death, when their folds became as gory as the ground over which we bore them, and, though reddened and stained with the smoke and blood of battle, they still maintained their position in the front. They waved together here when a Continent was at stake; they flashed in the Wilderness amid a revel of death; they were the first flags planted on the angle at Spotsylvania; and at each and every place, begirt by patriotism and battalioned by valor, they never wavered, never faltered, never quailed until they blazed in the sunlight of victory at Appomattox."

Denis F. Bourke, at the dedication of Irish Brigade monuments at Gettysburg, after the war.
(Source: *The Irish Brigade*, by Steven J. Wright)

Above: *Monument at Gettysburg of the 2nd Brigade, 1st Division, II Army Corps. The fallen soldier on the monument graphically portrays the casualties suffered by the already greatly under-strength brigade.*

Left: *"Return of the Flags, 1865," by Thomas Waterman Wood, showing the grizzled veterans of the brigade returning to New York City in July 1865. The flags are incorrectly portrayed as the First colors, not the Second colors that the unit actually carried on their return. The painting now hangs at West Point.*

"Perhaps the best known of any brigade organization, it having made an unusual reputation for dash and gallantry. The remarkable precision of its evolutions under fire, its desperate attack on the impregnable wall at Marye's Heights; its never failing promptness on every field; and its long continuous service, made for it a name inseparable from the history of the war."

William F. Fox describing the Irish Brigade in his *Regimental Losses in the American Civil War, 1861-1865*

References

Introduction

1 Farwell, Byron, *The Encyclopedia of Nineteenth-Century Land Warfare*, New York, W. W. Norton & Co., 2001, pgs 425-426
2 Ibid, p. 550
3 McDonald, JoAnna M., *The Faces of Irish Civil War Soldiers*, Redondo Beach, CA, Rank and File Publications, 1999, p. II
4 Woodhead, Henry, editor, *Echoes of Glory, Arms and Equipment of the Union*, Alexandria, VA, Time-Life Books, 1991, p. 274
5 Seagrave, Pia Seija, editor, *The History of the Irish Brigade*, Fredericksburg, VA, Sergeant Kirkland's Museum and Historical Society, 1997, p. 11
6 Lonn, Ella, *Foreigners in the Union Army and Navy*, New York, Greenwood Press, pgs 117-118, 121
7 Ibid, pgs 118-120
8 Ibid, p. 125
9 Ibid, pgs 646-647
10 Ellis, Thomas T., MD, *Leaves from the Diary of an Army Surgeon*, New York, John Bradburn, 1863, p. 54

Chapter 1

1 Seagrave, op. cit. pgs 14-16
2 Ibid, pgs 17-18
3 Warner, Ezra, J., *Generals in Blue*, Baton Rouge, LA, Louisiana State University Press, 1964, pgs 93-94
4 Seagrave, op. cit. pgs 26-29
5 Faust, Patricia L., editor, *Historical Times Illustrated Encyclopedia of the Civil War*, New York, Harper & Row, 1986, pgs 165-166
6 Lonn, Ella, *Foreigners in the Union Army and Navy*, New York, Greenwood Press, 1969, p. 201.
7 Seagrave, op cit. p. 34
8 Faust, op. cit. p. 166
9 Warner, op. cit. pgs 317-318
10 Conyngham, David Power (Lawrence Frederick Kohl, editor), *The Irish Brigade and Its Campaigns*, New York, Fordham University Press, 1994, p. 532
11 Lonn, op. cit. pgs 201-202
12 Conyngham, op. cit. p. 535
13 Faust, op. cit. p. 463
14 Warner, op. cit. pgs 317-318
15 O'Brien, Kevin E., editor, *My Life in the Irish Brigade. The Civil War Memoirs of Private William McCarter, 116th Pennsylvania Infantry*, Campbell, CA, Savas Publishing Co., 1996, p. 16
16 Ibid, pgs 70-71

17 Dyer, Frederick H., *A Compendium of the War of the Rebellion*, Dayton, OH, The National Historical Society and the Press of Morningside Bookshop, 1979, p. 288
18 Sparks, David S., editor, *Inside Lincoln's Army. The Diary of General Marsena Rudolph Patrick, Provost Marshal General, Army of the Potomac*, New York, Thomas Yoseloff, publisher, 1964, pgs 414-415.
19 Conyngham, op. cit. p. 548
20 Ibid, p. 558
21 Seagrave, op. cit. pgs 135-136
22 Ibid, pgs 170-173
23 Warner, op. cit. pgs 465-466
24 Conyngham, op. cit. pgs xviii-xxvi

Chapter 2

1 Conyngham, op. cit. after p. 488
2 Miller, Francis Trevelyan, *The Photographic History of the Civil War*, 5 vols. Secaucus, NJ, The Blue & Grey Press, 1987, Vol. 3, pgs 76-77
3 Seagrave, op. Cit. p 58
4 Coates, Earl J., McAfee, Michael J., and Troiani, Don, *Regiments and Uniforms of the Civil War*, Mechanicsburg, PA, Stackpole Books, 2002, pgs 40, 59
5 Mulholland, St. Clair A., *The Story of the 116th Regiment Pennsylvania Infantry*, Gaithersburg, MD, Olde Soldier Books, Inc. 1991, p. 33
6 Coates, McAfee and Troiani, op. cit., pgs 48-49
7 Conyngham, op. cit., after p. 488
8 Ibid, after p. 488
9 Woodhead, Henry, editor, *Echoes of Glory, Arms and Equipment of The Union*, Alexandria, VA, Time-Life Books, 1991, p. 172
10 Seagrave, op. cit. p. 87
11 Corby, William, C.S.C. (Lawrence Frederick Kohl, editor), *Memoirs of Chaplain Life, Three Years With the Irish Brigade in the Army of the Potomac*, New York, Fordham University Press, 1992, p. 375
12 McAfee, Michael J., and Langellier, John P., *Billy Yank, The Uniform of the Union Army, 1861-1865*, London, Greenhill Books and PA, Stackpole Books, 1996, pgs 56-57
13 O'Brien, Kevin E., editor, *My Life in the Irish Brigade: The Civil War Memoirs of Private William McCarter, 116th Pennsylvania Infantry*, Campbell, CA, Savas Publishing Company, 1996, p. 182

14 Reilly, Robert M., *United States Military Small Arms 1816-1865*, Highland Park, NJ, The Gun Room Press, 1970, pgs 21-23
15 Seagrave, op. cit. pgs 177-181
16 Mowbray, Stuart C., editor, *Civil War Arms Purchases and Deliveries, a reprint of Executive Document 99*, Lincoln, RI, Andrew Mowbray Publishers, 2000, p. 755
17 Mulholland, op. cit. p. 30
18 Seagrave, op. cit. p. 179
19 Phillips, Stanley S., *Excavated Artifacts from Battlefields and Campsites of the Civil War 1861-1865*, Supplement 1, Lanham, MD, S. S. Phillips and Assc., 1980, p. 89
20 Coates, McAfee and Troiani, op. cit. p. 44
21 Seagrave, op. cit. pgs 186-193
22 Conyngham, op. cit. pgs 55-57
23 Lysy, Peter J., *Blue for the Union & Green for Ireland*, South Bend, IN, Mossberg and Company, Inc.2001, pgs 8-15
24 www.28thmass.org/Flags/Flags.htm

Chapter 3

1 Seagrave, op. cit. p. 16
2 Athearn, Robert G., *Thomas Francis Meagher: An Irish Revolutionary in America*, New York, Arno Press, 1976, pgs 12-13
3 Seagrave, op. cit., p. 18
4 Ibid, p. 19
5 Lonn, op. cit. p. 118
6 Ibid, p. 119
7 Athearn, op. cit. p. 92
8 Seagrave, op. cit. p. 22
9 Athearn, op. cit. p. 95
10 Ibid, p.97
11 Seagrave, op. cit. p. 52
12 Athearn, op. cit. p. 99
13 Warner, op. cit. pgs 444-445.
14 Athearn, op. cit. p. 100
15 Seagrave, op. cit. p. 54
16 Warner, op. cit. pgs 444-445
17 Lysy, op. cit. p. 7
18 Conyngham, op. cit. p. 57
19 Athearn, op cit. p. 109
20 Conyngham, op. cit. pgs 94-96
21 Ibid, pgs 113-114

Chapter 4

1 Cullen, Joseph P., *The Peninsula Campaign, 1862*, Harrisburg, PA, Stackpole Books, 1973, p. 15
2 Conyngham, op. cit. p.146
3 Cullen, op. cit. p. 54
4 Corby, op. cit. pgs 59-60
5 Conyngham, op. cit. Pgs. 150-151
6 Ibid, p. 161
7 Athearn, op. cit. pgs 110-111
8 Cullen, op. cit., p. 95
9 Conyngham, op. cit. p. 186
10 Ibid, pgs 184-185

11 Ibid, p 198
12 Corby, op. cit. p. 75
13 Woodhead, Henry, series director, The Civil War: Lee Takes Command, Alexandria, VA, Time Life Books, Inc., p. 73
14 Conyngham, op. cit. p. 239
15 Athearn, op. cit. pgs 115-116
16 Priest, John Michael, *Antietam: The Soldier's Battle*, New York and Oxford, Oxford University Press, 1989, p 160
17 Conyngham, op. cit. 305-306
18 Priest, op. cit. p. 160
19 Conyngham, op. cit. p. 306
20 Priest, op. cit. pgs 180-182
21 Ibid, p. 182
22 Frasssanito, William A., *Antietam: The Photographic Legacy of America's Bloodiest Day*, New York, Charles Scribner's Sons, 1978, p. 208
23 Athearn, op. cit. pgs 117-118
24 Priest, op. cit. p. 335
25 Conyngham, op. cit. p. 319
26 Ibid, p. 324
27 Ibid, p. 327
28 Ibid, p.
29 Ibid, p. 577
30 Athearn, op. cit. p. 119
31 Conyngham, op. cit. pgs 338-339
32 O'Brien, op cit. p. 167
33 Athearn, op. cit. p. 121
34 O'Brien, op. cit. p. 168
35 Athearn, op.cit. p. 120
36 Conyngham, op. cit. p. 350
37 Lysy, op. cit. p. 8
38 Athearn, op. cit. p. 123
39 Conyngham, op. cit. pgs 372-380
40 Corby, op. cit. p. 29
41 Mulholland, op. cit. pgs 109-110
42 Athearn, p. 125

Chapter 5

1 Conyngham, op. cit. pgs 406-407
2 Mulholland, op. cit. p. 129
3 Ibid, p. 135
4 Corby, op. cit. pgs 182-184
5 Mulholland, op. cit. p. 164
6 Conyngham, op. cit. pgs 427-436
7 Mulholland, op. cit. p. 168
8 Conyngham, op. cit. pgs 439-440
9 Mulholland, op. cit. pgs 198-202
10 Ibid. pgs 223-224
11 Ibid. pgs 246-247
12 Conyngham, op. cit. pgs 482-484
13 Ibid, p. 524
14 Seagrave, op. cit. p. 56
15 Lysy, op. cit. p. 12
16 Walker, Francis A., *History of the Second Army Corps*, New York, Charles Scribner's Sons, 1886, p. 543

Bibliography

Acken, J. Gregory, Editor, *Inside the Army of the Potomac, The Civil War Experience of Captain Francis Adams Donaldson*, Mechanicsburg, PA, Stackpole Books, 1998

Amann, William Frayne, Editor, *Personnel of the Civil War*, 2 Vols. New York, Thomas Yoseloff, 1961.

Athearn, Robert G., *Thomas Francis Meagher: An Irish Revolutionary in America*. New York, Arno Press, 1976

Beyer, W. F. and Keydel, O. F, Editors, *Deeds of Valor. How America's Civil War Heroes Won The Congressional Medal of Honor*, New York, Smithmark Publishers, 2000

Boatner, Mark M., *The Civil War Dictionary*, New York, Davis McKay and Company.1959

Coates, Earl J., McAfee, Michael J. and Troiani, Don, *Regiments & Uniforms of the Civil War*, Mechanicsburg, PA, Stackpole Books, 2002

Conyngham, David Power (Lawrence Frederick Kohl, Editor), *The Irish Brigade and Its Campaigns*, New York, Fordham University Press, 1994.

Corby, William, C.S.C. (Lawrence Frederick Kohl, Editor), *Memoirs of Chaplain Life, Three Years with the Irish Brigade in the Army of the Potomac*, New York, Fordham University Press, 1992.

Cullen, Joseph P., *The Peninsula Campaign*, 1862, Harrisburg, PA, Stackpole Books, 1973.

Dyer, Frederick P., *A Compendium of the War of the Rebellion*, 2 Vols., Dayton, OH, The National Historical Society in cooperation with The Press of Morningside Bookshop, 1979.

Farwell, Byron, *The Encyclopedia of Nineteenth-Century Land Warfare*, New York, W. W. Norton & Company, 2001.

Ellis, Thomas T., M.D., *Leaves from the Diary of an Army Surgeon*, New York, John Bradburn, 1863.

Faust, Patricia L., Editor, *Historical Times Illustrated Encyclopedia of the Civil War*, New York, Harper & Row, 1986.

Frassanito, William A., *Antietam, The Photographic Legacy of America's Bloodiest Day*, New York, Charles Scribner's Sons, 1978.

Livermore, Thomas L., *Numbers and Losses in the Civil War in America: 1861-1865*, Bloomington, Indiana University Press, 1957, New York, Kraus Reprint Co., 1969.

Lonn, Ella, *Foreigners in the Union Army and Navy*, New York, Greenwood Press, 1969

Lysy, Peter J. *Blue for the Union & Green for Ireland*, South Bend, Indiana, Mossberg and Company, Inc. 2001.

Manning, Robert, Editor-in-Chief, *Above and Beyond, A History of the Medal of Honor from the Civil War to Vietnam*, Boston, Boston Publishing Company, 1985.

McAfee, Michael J. and Langellier, John P., *Billy Yank, The Uniform of the Union Army, 1861-1865*, London, Greenhill Books and Mechanicburg, PA, Stackpole Books, 1996

McDonald, JoAnna M., *The Faces of Irish Civil War Soldiers*, Redondo Beach, CA, Rank and File Publications, 1999.

Miller, Francis Trevelyan, Editor-in-Chief, *The Photographic History of the Civil War*, 10 Vols. New York, The Review of Reviews Co., 1912.

Mulholland, St. Clair A., Brevet Major General, *The Story of the 116th Regiment, Pennsylvania Infantry*, Philadelphia, PA, F. McManus, Jr. & Company, Printers, 1903.

O'Brien, Kevin E. *My Life in the Irish Brigade. The Civil War Memoirs of Private William McCarter, 116th Pennsylvania Infantry*. Campbell, CA, Savas Publishing Co. 1996

Priest, John Michael, *Antietam, The Soldiers'* Battle, Shippensburg, PA, White Mane Publishing Company, Inc., 1989

Seagrave, Pia Seija, Ph.D., Editor, *The History of the Irish Brigade, A Collection of Historical Essays*, Fredericksburg, VA, Sergeant Kirkland's Museum and Historical Society, Inc. Revised Edition, 1997.

Sears, Stephen W., *Chancellorsville*, New York, Houghton Mifflin Company, 1996.

Sifkasis, Stewart, *Who Was Who In The Civil War*, New York, Facts on File, 1988

Sparks, David S., Editor, *Inside Lincoln's Army. The Diary of General Marsena Rudolph Patrick, Provost Marshal General; Army of the Potomac*, New York, Thomas Yoseloff, Publisher, 1964

U. S. War Department., *The War of the Rebellion: A Compilation of the Official Records of the Union and Confederate Armies*, 128 Vols., Washington, DC, U. S. Government Printing Office, 1880-1901.

Walker, Francis A., *History of the Second Army Corps*, New York, Charles Scribner's Sons, 1886,

Warner, Ezra J., *Generals in Blue*, Baton Rouge, LA, Louisiana State University Press, 1964.

Woodhead, Henry, Series Director, *The Civil War. Lee Takes Command*, Alexandria, VA, Time-Life Books, 1984.

Woodhead, Henry, Editor, Echoes of Glory, *Arms and Equipment of the Union*, Alexandria, VA, Time-Life Books, 1991

Wright, Steven J., *The Irish Brigade*, Springfield, PA, Steven Wright Publishing, 1992.

Index